Cryptocurrency Simplified:

A Beginner's Guide to Digital Assets, Risk Awareness, and Real-World Insights

Step into the world of cryptocurrency with this comprehensive guide designed to make digital assets easy to understand. This book explores both the opportunities and risks, empowering you to make smart, informed decisions in the digital economy.

DENISE D. MEJIA

This book is provided for educational and informational purposes only. It does not constitute financial, investment, legal, or professional advice. Readers should conduct their own research and consult qualified professionals before making financial or investment decisions.

Cryptocurrency and digital asset markets involve risk, including potential loss of capital. The author and publisher disclaim any liability for losses or damages arising from the use of this information.

First Edition

ISBN: 979-8-218-93325-8

Published by CryptoLens

Acknowledgments

I owe immense gratitude to Blockchain Professor Ayesha Kiani of New York University and COO of Monarq Asset Management. Her rigorous peer review and academic insights into the complexities of blockchain technology were invaluable, ensuring the technical accuracy and clarity of this guide. Thank you for your support and pioneering work in this financial frontier.

Table of Contents

Author's Note

Dedication

I dedicate this book to the "everyday person"—not just those in FinTech, but also to the curious, the cautious, and the skeptics. To my friends, family, and anyone who has ever wondered what "Bitcoin" really means or how the world of crypto works—this is for you.

Introduction

This guide offers a clear and accessible introduction to cryptocurrency—from its core concepts and key terms to real-world examples that make digital assets easier to grasp. It explores both the opportunities and the risks, helping readers understand how cryptocurrencies function, what drives their value, and how to navigate the market safely. By the end, you'll have a strong foundation in crypto history, market mechanics, adoption trends, and security best practices, empowering you to protect yourself from scams and misinformation.

"Arm yourself with knowledge so you can take advantage of opportunities when the time comes."

-Denise D. Mejía

Chapter 1

Introduction to Cryptocurrency

What's the Purpose of Cryptocurrency?

Imagine a world where money isn't controlled by a central bank or a government—a world where every transaction is recorded on a transparent, public ledger for anyone to see, making it difficult to cheat the system. This isn't a sci-fi fantasy; it's the reality of cryptocurrency.

Cryptocurrency isn't just a digital replacement for the cash in your wallet—it's a new way to hold and move value that exists entirely online. There are no bills to fold; it is pure data, a revolutionary form of payment built on a groundbreaking technology known as the blockchain.

To access and manage your digital wealth, you use a digital wallet, which acts as your personal vault. Inside this vault are your cryptocurrency keys—unique, private codes that prove ownership of your cryptocurrency.

Although cryptocurrency exists digitally, it is not limited to online use. It can be spent where accepted, traded on global exchanges, or converted into traditional currency through regulated platforms. In some regions, crypto ATMs allow users to exchange digital assets for cash, connecting crypto to everyday financial systems.

Crypto assets are often referred to as a "project" because they involve a combination of technological development, financial innovation, and community-driven efforts. Like other projects, crypto projects have goals, plans, and a vision for their impact.

What Crypto Is Not

Cryptocurrency is often discussed in bold and dramatic terms, which can make it challenging for newcomers to separate facts from assumptions. One helpful way to build clarity is to understand what crypto is not intended to be. While digital assets have opened new possibilities, they do not promise guaranteed returns. Like any financial system, outcomes depend on market conditions, usage, and broader economic factors.

Crypto is also not anonymous by default, nor is it meant to replace traditional finance entirely. Many blockchain activities are traceable, particularly when they intersect with regulated platforms.

Rather than eliminating existing systems, crypto introduces alternative tools that can complement them. Recognizing these boundaries helps you approach digital assets with realistic expectations and a clearer sense of how crypto fits into today's financial landscape.

Cryptocurrency replaces blind trust in institutions with verifiable trust in technology, giving you more control over how value is stored and transferred. It is more than a new form of money; it represents a new chapter in financial history. Are you ready to explore it?

The diagram below illustrates a simple Bitcoin exchange between Mario and Emma.

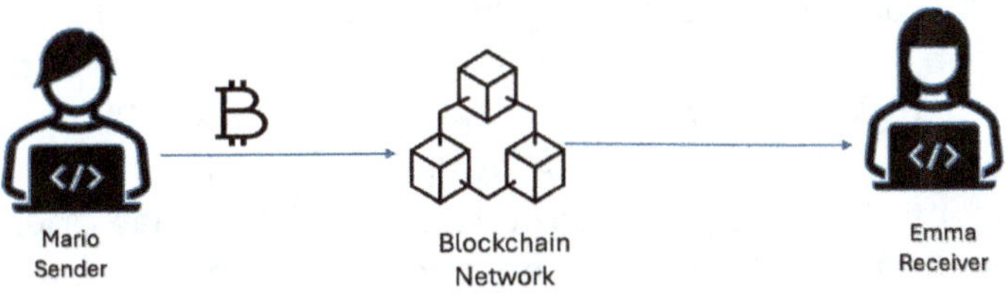

Takeaway: Cryptocurrency is entirely digital—it isn't physical like paper money, certificates, or traditional coins. It is stored on blockchain networks and accessed through personal digital keys. However, some companies create physical coins with a private key embedded, but these are only representations of cryptocurrency, not cryptocurrency itself.

A Brief History of Cryptocurrency

The history of cryptocurrency is both innovative and unconventional. Early ideas that helped shape modern digital currencies emerged in 1983, when cryptographer David Chaum introduced the concept of electronic cash—an early attempt to enable secure digital payments using cryptography.

The true birth of cryptocurrency, however, occurred in 2008, when an unknown individual or group using the pseudonym Satoshi Nakamoto published the white paper *"Bitcoin: A Peer-to-Peer Electronic Cash System."* The paper proposed a decentralized form of digital money—one that operates without central banks or intermediaries and relies on a public, tamper-resistant ledger now known as the blockchain.

Satoshi Nakamoto remained active in Bitcoin's development until December 2010, after which they disappeared from public view. To this day, their identity remains unknown, fueling speculation and debate within the crypto community. Despite various claims, no one has definitively proven they are Satoshi Nakamoto.

For some, it sounded like a joke, or something straight out of a fiction book. At the time, Bitcoin was widely dismissed as unrealistic or even fictional.

The idea of replacing physical money with purely digital currency—especially one not issued or backed by governments—was difficult for many to accept. This skepticism helped shape the controversy surrounding cryptocurrency, a debate that continues today.

Cryptocurrency adoption initially came from cryptography enthusiasts and software developers. Bitcoin officially launched in 2009 as open-source (publicly accessible) software, and the first recorded commercial transaction took place in 2010, when programmer **Laszlo Hanyecz** paid **10,000 BTC** for two pizzas. At the time, Bitcoin was worth less than a cent per coin. By December 2025, Bitcoin's price had approached $90,000, making those two pizzas worth hundreds of millions of dollars—a reminder of how dramatically the market has evolved. In hindsight, given today's value of Bitcoin, that purchase wouldn't just be buying dinner; it would be equivalent to **buying the entire pizza franchise.**

Bitcoin was soon followed by other digital assets known as **altcoins,** beginning in **2011.** These alternative cryptocurrencies aimed to improve upon Bitcoin's limitations or introduce new functionality. You may have heard of Litecoin, XRP, and Ethereum. **Ethereum** changed the game by adding **smart contracts,** which allowed people to use crypto for much more than just sending money. While Bitcoin continues to dominate the market by capitalization, altcoins play a significant role in innovation across the ecosystem.

In 2017, Initial Coin Offerings (ICOs) emerged as a new fundraising method, allowing blockchain projects to raise capital by issuing digital tokens. While this accelerated innovation, it also led to widespread fraud and scams, prompting regulatory scrutiny—particularly from the U.S. Securities and Exchange Commission (SEC).

A major milestone occurred in **September 2021**, when El Salvador became the first country to adopt Bitcoin as **legal tender**, alongside the U.S. dollar. The government created a national digital app to make it easy to pay for goods and services with Bitcoin. It was the first time a country tried using crypto as a main form of money.

In **2024**, the SEC approved the first **spot Bitcoin Exchange-Traded Funds (ETFs)** in the United States, allowing investors to gain direct exposure to Bitcoin through traditional financial markets.

By **April 2025**, global cryptocurrency market capitalization was estimated at approximately **$3.6 trillion**, reflecting the industry's rapid growth and increasing integration into global finance.

Today, the cryptocurrency market offers a wide range of assets and opportunities, including established cryptocurrencies, altcoins, stablecoins, Decentralized Finance (DeFi), gaming, virtual environments, lending platforms, and privacy-focused coins. The crypto landscape remains dynamic and continuously evolving, requiring investors to stay informed, adaptable, and cautious.

Takeaway: Cryptocurrency did not emerge overnight. It evolved over decades of experimentation, skepticism, and technological breakthroughs. While early ideas like Bitcoin challenged traditional views of money and sparked rapid innovation, they also introduced volatility, speculation, and new risks—setting the stage for both the opportunities and challenges that define today's crypto ecosystem.

The timeline below highlights key milestones in the evolution of cryptocurrency.

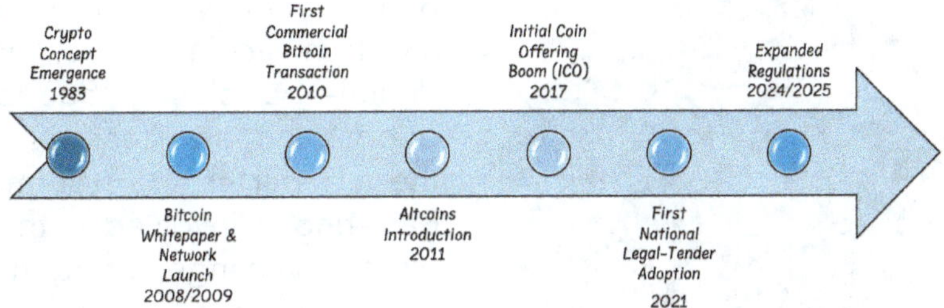

What Is the Difference Between Traditional Currency and Cryptocurrency?

Before money existed in any form—coins, paper, or digital—people traded goods and services using the **barter system.** Bartering involved the direct exchange of items based on mutual agreement of value. For example, a farmer might trade bushels of wheat for a pot made by a potter.

The first known coins originated in Lydia (modern-day Turkey) around 600 BCE. Paper currency appeared much later, in China during the Tang Dynasty (618–907 CE). In contrast, cryptocurrency is still in its early stages, with its modern origins dating back to the early 2000s and the creation of Bitcoin in 2008.

Traditional currency, also known as **fiat currency**, is issued and regulated by central banks such as the U.S. Federal Reserve or the European Central Bank. Fiat currency exists in physical form (coins and paper bills) and in digital form through banking systems. Cryptocurrencies, on the other hand, are **decentralized** and are not controlled by any government or central authority. They operate on **blockchain technology**, a digital ledger that records transactions in linked blocks across a network of computers.

Central banks can print more fiat money to increase supply, which can lead to inflation. In contrast, many cryptocurrencies have a **fixed supply.**

For example, Bitcoin has a maximum supply cap of **21 million coins,** as defined by its underlying protocol. This built-in limit is designed to create scarcity.

In general, traditional currency is more stable and widely accepted because it is backed by governments and financial institutions. Cryptocurrencies, while more volatile, offer new possibilities for innovation, financial inclusion, and global digital transactions.

Takeaway: Cryptocurrency represents a major evolution in the history of money. Unlike traditional fiat currency, it is fully digital, decentralized, and powered by miners and validators instead of central banks. While crypto remains volatile and still evolving, it offers significant opportunities through innovations such as altcoins, stablecoins, Non-Fungible Tokens (NFTs), and Decentralized Finance (DeFi).

Fiat Currency vs. Cryptocurrency Comparison

Question	Fiat Currency	Cryptocurrency
Who controls it?	Central banks and governments	Decentralized network (no single authority)
Is it physical?	Yes (cash, coins) and digital	Digital only
How is it created?	Printed or issued by central banks	Created through mining or staking
Supply limit?	Unlimited (can be printed)	Usually limited (e.g., Bitcoin = 21 million)
How are transactions verified?	Banks and payment processors	Blockchain network and validators
Transaction speed	Minutes to days	Seconds to minutes
Availability	Limited to banking hours	24/7 worldwide
Can transactions be reversed?	Often yes (refunds/chargebacks possible)	Usually no (transactions are final)
Transparency	Low (private bank records)	High (public blockchain ledger)
Security responsibility	Mostly handled by banks	Mostly handled by the user (wallets and keys)
Global transfers	Slower and often costlier cross-border	Typically faster cross-border
Access required	Usually requires a bank account	Requires a wallet and internet access
Examples	USD, EUR, JPY	BTC, ETH, USDC

Chapter 2

How Does Cryptocurrency Work?

Cryptocurrency uses cryptography to secure transactions and control the creation of new units. The word *"crypto"* refers to advanced encryption techniques used to verify transactions and safely transfer funds between users. At the core of this ecosystem is the blockchain network, which acts as a shared digital record-keeping system distributed across a network of computers.

The blockchain stores data in blocks that are linked together, making it extremely difficult to alter information once it has been recorded. It can be compared to a Google Docs file that everyone can view, but no one can change without others noticing—every update is visible and permanently logged.

Blockchain technology was designed with security, transparency, and integrity in mind. While Bitcoin was the first major use of blockchain, the technology itself is much broader and continues to evolve.

Today, blockchain supports the creation, transfer, and management of many types of digital assets.

Blockchain records transactions in a transparent, tamper-resistant way, but it does not eliminate risk. Most losses in crypto come from human error, scams, or weak platforms—not from the blockchain itself.

The cryptocurrency ecosystem is a decentralized digital financial system made up of several key components, including blockchain networks, cryptocurrencies, miners and validators, wallets, exchanges, and decentralized applications. These elements work together to enable transparent peer-to-peer[1] transactions, with each component playing an important role in the security, functionality, and growth of the ecosystem.

Takeaway: Cryptocurrency is powered by blockchain technology, a shared digital ledger that records transactions transparently. Together with cryptography, wallets, and decentralized networks, it allows people to exchange value directly without relying on banks or central authorities.

---

[1] "peer-to-peer" is a decentralized network architecture where all participants (nodes/users) are equally privileged and share the workload. It allows two individuals to interact directly with each other without the need for an intermediate central authority.
https://www.blockchain-council.org/blockchain/peer-to-peer/

The Crypto Ecosystem

If you are considering investing in the crypto market, it helps to understand the components involved and how they connect. The cryptocurrency ecosystem is made up of many interdependent elements, including blockchain, coins, tokens, wallets, mining, staking, transactions, exchanges, investing, rewards, regulators, decentralization, Decentralized Autonomous Organizations (DAOs), risks, and tokenomics. Each element plays a specific role in supporting the broader system and enabling digital value to move without relying on traditional financial institutions. Together, these components form a decentralized, transparent, and highly innovative financial ecosystem.

Tokenomics refers to the study of a cryptocurrency project's economic design, including how tokens are created, distributed, used, and governed. It combines *token* and *economics* and helps investors understand supply, incentives, and long-term sustainability.

Cryptocurrencies are entirely digital and exist only on blockchain networks, where they are stored, transferred, and traded. They can represent money, digital property, access rights, governance power, or ownership in a project. Their value is determined by decentralization, utility, market demand, and broader economic conditions.

The figure below illustrates the crypto ecosystem and the key components.

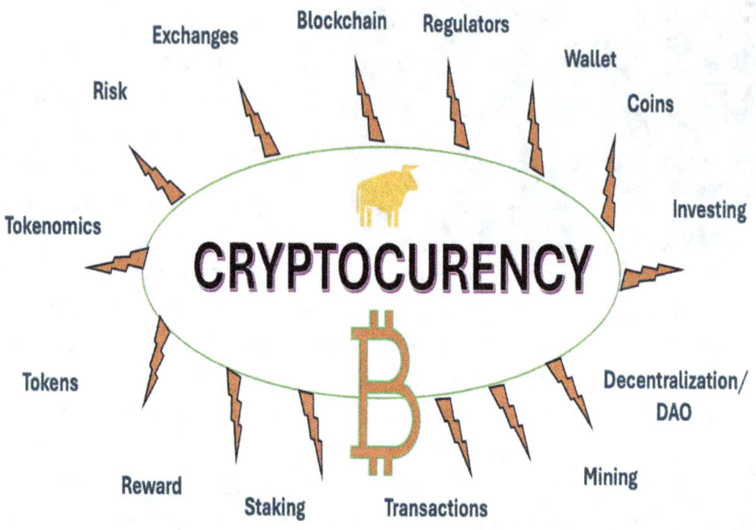

How are Key Components of the Crypto Ecosystem Related to Each Other?

The cryptocurrency ecosystem functions as a network of interconnected systems, each contributing to how value is created, transferred, and managed:

- Coins are the main form of digital money on a blockchain. They are used for payments, transaction fees, and to keep the network running by rewarding those who maintain it.

- Blockchain is the foundational layer that records transactions and stores data in a distributed ledger shared across many computers.

- Miners and validators confirm transactions and maintain the network, ensuring it continues to operate as intended.

- Wallets allow users to store, send, and receive cryptocurrencies, acting as the gateway to the ecosystem.

- Exchanges serve as marketplaces where users buy, sell, and trade cryptocurrencies, bridging traditional finance and crypto markets.

- Smart contracts enable automated, rule-based transactions without intermediaries and power decentralized applications (dApps) and DeFi platforms.

- Tokens and NFTs expand blockchain functionality beyond payments, enabling ownership, access, and digital identity.

- DAOs and governance systems allow communities to vote and manage projects collectively without central control.

- Regulators influence how crypto operates legally, shaping compliance requirements and consumer protections.

- Tokenomics provides insight into supply, incentives, and sustainability, helping investors evaluate projects.

Behind the scenes, the crypto ecosystem also includes infrastructure providers, data oracles, scaling networks, custodians, and security services that help blockchains run efficiently, securely, and at global scale.

Blockchain Technology Basics

You don't need to be a blockchain expert to understand how the crypto market works. While this section is technical in nature, the goal of this section is simply to help you understand what's happening behind the scenes and how the different pieces of the crypto ecosystem fit together.

Before diving deeper, it's important to understand the difference between coins and tokens, since these terms are often used interchangeably but mean different things. Coins are digital money that exist on their own blockchain network. For example, Bitcoin is used on the Bitcoin network, and Ether is used on the Ethereum network. Coins are mainly used for payments, transaction fees, and keeping the network running. Tokens, on the other hand, are created on top of existing blockchains and can serve many purposes beyond just money. Depending on how they are programmed through smart contracts, tokens can represent currency, ownership, access rights, voting power, or even real-world assets.

Tokens often act as keys that unlock other parts of the crypto ecosystem. Well-known examples include USDC and DAI, which are tokens used as stable forms of value and exchange.

Coins, by contrast, are native to their own blockchains and are essential for network operations. Bitcoin is primarily used as a digital currency, while Ether is used to pay transaction fees (known as "gas fees") and power applications on the Ethereum network.

At the center of all of this is the blockchain, which records transactions and tracks digital assets across a distributed network of computers. As described in *"Bitcoin: A Peer-to-Peer Electronic Cash System"*, the blockchain operates without control from central banks or governments, making it decentralized. Information is stored in blocks that are linked together in chronological order, forming a chain. Each block references the one before it, using cryptographic hashes, making it extremely difficult to alter past records without changing every block that follows.

This design is what makes blockchain immutable—once information is recorded, it cannot be easily changed or deleted. As a result, transactions are generally final. Sending cryptocurrency to someone's wallet is like handing someone cash in person: once it's sent, it cannot be retrieved. Because there is no central authority to reverse or cancel transactions, users are strongly advised to double-check wallet addresses before sending funds.

Beyond cryptocurrency, blockchain technology supports many other real-world applications.

It is used in supply chain management to track products, in identity verification to reduce fraud, in healthcare to share records securely, and in voting systems to improve transparency. It is also used for public record keeping, copyright management, and real estate transactions, where ownership can be verified digitally without relying on a central authority.

Blockchains generally fall into three main categories: **public, private, and consortium.** Public blockchains, such as Bitcoin and Ethereum, are open networks where anyone can participate and view transactions. Private blockchains are used by organizations that restrict access to approved members, often for internal operations. Consortium blockchains are governed by multiple organizations that share control, offering a balance between transparency and permissioned access.

Some networks also use hybrid blockchain models, which combine elements of both public and private systems. In these cases, certain data is publicly verifiable, while sensitive information is restricted to authorized parties. This flexibility allows blockchain technology to adapt to many different use cases across industries.

Why Are There So Many Blockchain Networks?

It can be confusing to see so many different blockchains when the technology itself has already been created. To understand why, think of blockchain networks like **different types of power tools.** Even though we have electricity, we don't use a massive industrial drill to hang a small picture frame, and we don't use a tiny screwdriver to build a skyscraper. Different jobs need different tools.

Some networks focus on security and decentralization, while others emphasize speed, low transaction costs, or specialized features. Understanding this diversity helps beginners see blockchains not as competitors in a single race, but as tools designed for different purposes within a growing digital ecosystem.

The Role of Miners and Validators in the Ecosystem

When a user sends cryptocurrency to someone else or transfers data on a blockchain, that transaction is broadcast to a network of computers called **nodes**. These nodes maintain the blockchain by checking transactions and making sure they follow the network's rules.

On the Bitcoin network, transactions are verified using a process called **Proof of Work (PoW)**. In this system, miners compete to solve complex mathematical puzzles to add new blocks to the blockchain. Solving these puzzles requires large amounts of computing power and electricity, which is why PoW is often criticized for its energy consumption. Once a miner successfully solves the puzzle, the block is added to the blockchain, and the miner is rewarded with newly created coins and transaction fees.

Other blockchains use a different system called **Proof of Stake (PoS)**. Instead of relying on computing power, PoS relies on participants called **validators**, who lock up (or *stake*) a certain amount of cryptocurrency as collateral.

By staking their assets, validators earn the right to help confirm transactions and add new blocks to the chain.

The Ethereum network uses Proof of Stake as its consensus mechanism because it is far more energy-efficient than PoW. In PoS systems, validators are often selected based on how much cryptocurrency they have staked. This can sometimes concentrate power among those who hold large amounts of tokens, raising concerns about fairness and decentralization.

Validators are responsible for checking transactions and proposing new blocks. If a validator behaves dishonestly or validates incorrect data, the network can penalize them by taking away part or all their staked funds. This penalty is known as **slashing**, and it helps keep validators honest.

Whether through mining or staking, miners and validators are essential to the blockchain ecosystem. They ensure that transactions are valid, that the network continues to run smoothly, and that new blocks are added to the ledger. In return for their work, they receive rewards in the form of newly minted coins and transaction fees, which is how new cryptocurrency enters circulation.

What Are Exchanges?

Exchanges play a vital role in the cryptocurrency ecosystem because they connect the decentralized world of crypto with the traditional financial system. They provide centralized or decentralized platforms where users can buy, sell, and trade digital assets. Without exchanges, most people would have no easy way to enter or exit the crypto market.

A crypto exchange is not the same thing as a blockchain network. A blockchain is the underlying system that records and verifies transactions, while an exchange is a service that helps people buy, sell, and trade cryptocurrencies. Exchanges act as intermediaries, similar to online brokerage platforms, making crypto more accessible without controlling the blockchain itself. Understanding this distinction helps explain why assets held on an exchange are subject to the exchange's rules, while assets stored in a personal wallet exist directly on the blockchain.

Exchanges provide liquidity, meaning they make it possible to quickly buy or sell cryptocurrencies without causing large price changes. They also allow users to convert crypto into other cryptocurrencies or into fiat money, such as U.S. dollars.

In addition, exchanges help introduce new tokens to the market and support price discovery, which is the process of determining a fair price based on supply and demand.

You can think of a crypto exchange like a stock market for digital assets. Just as the stock market lists many companies, a crypto exchange lists many cryptocurrencies and allows users to trade between them. These trading pairs, such as Bitcoin to Ethereum, give users more flexibility and help them diversify their portfolios.

Exchanges also act like marketplaces, similar to eBay or OfferUp, where buyers and sellers meet to trade directly. When users trade directly with each other, it's known as peer-to-peer (P2P) trading.

Some centralized exchanges, often called CEXs, operate more like banks by holding customer funds and offering services such as lending, borrowing, and earning interest.

Reputable exchanges add extra layers of protection by using security tools like multi-factor authentication and cold storage, where assets are kept offline to reduce the risk of hacking.

Takeaway: Exchanges are the entry point to the crypto world. They make it possible for everyday users to buy, sell, trade, and convert digital assets, connecting traditional money with the digital economy.

What Is Decentralized Finance (DeFi), and Why Does It Use Smart Contracts?

Decentralized Finance, or **DeFi**, is a financial system built on public blockchain networks. Its goal is to recreate traditional financial services—such as lending, borrowing, and trading—without relying on banks or other intermediaries. Instead, DeFi uses blockchain technology and smart contracts to allow people to interact directly with financial applications. Popular DeFi platforms include Aave, Compound, and Uniswap, where users can trade, lend, or earn interest on their crypto assets without going through a central institution.

At the heart of DeFi are **smart contracts**, sometimes called crypto contracts. These are computer programs that automatically execute actions when specific conditions are met. Instead of signing a paper agreement, the rules are written into code. For example, a smart contract might say, "If this payment is received, then release this asset."

Once the contract is created and stored on the blockchain, it runs on its own and is difficult to change. To make this more tangible, imagine Thomas sending $800 worth of ETH to a smart contract to buy an NFT. The contract automatically transfers the NFT to Thomas once the payment is confirmed—no bank, no lawyer, and no middleman involved. The code executes the agreement exactly as written. This automation can reduce costs, speed up transactions, and remove the need to trust a third party.

The idea of smart contracts is not new. It was first proposed in the 1990s by computer scientist Nick Szabo, but blockchain networks like Ethereum and Solana finally made the concept practical. These networks allow smart contracts to run decentralized applications, opening the door to new uses in finance, real estate, gaming, and digital ownership.

However, smart contracts are not risk-free. If there is an error in the code, it can be exploited. A well-known example is the 2016 DAO hack, where a flaw in a smart contract led to the theft of about $60 million. Once a smart contract is deployed, fixing mistakes is often difficult unless special upgrade features were built in from the start.

There are also legal and practical challenges. For example, if one person in Country A enters a smart contract with someone in Country B, it may be unclear which country's laws apply.

Costs can also be an issue. On networks like Ethereum, transactions can become expensive during busy periods, with "gas fees" sometimes reaching $50 or more. High fees and heavy network usage also raise environmental concerns.

What Is Tokenization of Real-World Assets (RWA)

Now that we have the blockchain—a shared digital record—we need something to record on it. Tokenization is the process of converting real-world value into a digital form so it can exist and move on a blockchain. In simple terms, tokenization takes a real-world asset and turns it into a digital token.

This digital token represents the legal rights and ownership of the asset. Whether the asset is a share of a company, a piece of art, real estate, or a gold bar, those rights are placed into a digital container that the blockchain can recognize, track, and transfer. Instead of moving the physical asset itself, the blockchain moves the token that represents it. For example, a commercial building can be tokenized so that each token represents a small ownership share of the property. Investors can buy, sell, or trade these tokens without needing to transfer the building itself.

Similarly, a gold bar stored in a vault can be tokenized, allowing people to own and trade digital tokens that represent ownership of that gold, while the physical asset remains stored in the vault. In this way, tokenization allows real-world assets to be owned, transferred, and managed digitally, making ownership more accessible, efficient, and transparent.

Advantages and Disadvantages of Decentralization

Advantages of Decentralization

In a decentralized network, transactions are verified by many independent participants instead of a single authority. This shared validation process increases transparency, because anyone can see what is happening on the network and verify activity for themselves. Decentralized applications, often called **dApps**, build on this idea by allowing people to interact directly with financial tools, services, or digital assets without relying on banks, payment processors, or technology companies as intermediaries.

Removing the middleman can reduce fees, eliminate delays, and lower the need to trust a third party with sensitive information. Because dApps are accessible from anywhere with an internet connection, they also promote financial inclusion and global participation.

In addition, decentralization limits censorship. No single entity can block transactions or control content, giving users more autonomy over their assets and data.

On blockchains like Ethereum, anyone can track transactions, wallet movements, and smart contract activity in real time. This level of openness is very different from traditional banking, where customers must rely on institutions and staff to approve or deny transactions. In decentralized systems, users control their funds directly through their private keys.

What Are Decentralized Autonomous Organizations (DAOs)?

Decentralized Autonomous Organizations, or DAOs, are groups that operate without centralized leadership. Instead of managers or executives, DAOs are governed by smart contracts and community voting. Members typically participate by holding governance tokens, which allow them to propose and vote on changes, funding decisions, or project direction.

In a DAO, rules are written into code, and decisions are made collectively. This structure allows communities to manage projects transparently and democratically, without relying on a central authority. DAOs play an important role in Decentralized Finance, blockchain governance, and open-source development.

Disadvantages of Decentralization

While decentralization offers many benefits, it also introduces challenges that beginners should understand. Scalability remains a major issue, as decentralized networks can process fewer transactions per second than centralized systems, which can lead to slow speeds and high fees during busy periods. Security risks also exist, especially when dApps contain coding errors that hackers can exploit.

Regulatory uncertainty is another concern. Laws around decentralized systems are still evolving, and it is not always clear which rules apply across borders. Blockchain interoperability is also limited. For example, an NFT created on the Ethereum network cannot easily be transferred to Solana because each blockchain uses different technical standards.

Adoption can be difficult because many users prefer familiar, centralized systems that offer customer support and the ability to reverse mistakes. In decentralized systems, transactions are usually final, which means sending funds to the wrong address can result in permanent loss.

Decentralized Finance (DeFi) protocols can be especially risky. Many rely heavily on speculation and market sentiment, which creates volatility and skepticism among investors. Governance can also be slow or unbalanced, since DAOs sometimes struggle to reach timely decisions when voting power is concentrated among a small group of token holders.

Energy consumption remains a concern for certain decentralized systems, particularly those using Proof-of-Work. In 2022, New York State introduced a temporary moratorium on crypto mining to reduce emissions from energy-intensive operations.

While some U.S. states like Texas and Wyoming are encouraging renewable energy use in mining, environmental impact remains a topic of ongoing regulatory attention. There is currently no unified global regulatory guidance. However, this topic remains a significant concern for regulators.

Takeaway: Decentralization gives users more control, transparency, and freedom—but it also removes safety nets. With greater power comes greater responsibility, and understanding the risks is just as important as understanding the technology.

What Is the Purpose of Oracles?

Smart contracts cannot access real-world information on their own. They can only read and act on data that already exists on the blockchain. This is where **oracles** come in. Oracles are services that bring real-world data onto the blockchain so smart contracts can react to events outside the digital world. The name "oracle" comes from ancient times, when oracles were trusted messengers that delivered knowledge from the outside world. In blockchain, oracles play a similar role—they act as trusted data messengers between the real world and smart contracts.

For example, if a smart contract needs to know the current price of Bitcoin, whether a flight was delayed, or if rainfall exceeded a certain amount, it cannot check that information by itself. An oracle fetches the data from reliable sources and delivers it to the blockchain so the contract can execute automatically. Without oracles, smart contracts would be limited to simple on-chain actions and could not support real-world applications like insurance, lending, or payments.

You can think of oracles as **apps on your phone that pull live data from the internet.** When you check the weather, track a package, or look up a stock price, your phone is using external data feeds. Oracles do the same thing for blockchains—they feed external data into smart contracts so they can make decisions automatically. For example, a travel insurance smart contract might use an oracle to confirm whether a flight was delayed. If the oracle reports a delay, the contract can automatically release a payment to the traveler without human involvement.

Oracles are widely used across industries. In finance, they provide real-time price data for cryptocurrencies and stocks, enabling automated trading, lending, and liquidations. In transportation, oracles can pull GPS data to verify delivery routes or confirm when a shipment arrives. In environmental monitoring, they can provide air quality or weather data to trigger contracts for farming or disaster relief. Even gaming and sports betting platforms use oracles to verify match results before paying out winnings.

One of the most well-known oracle networks is **Chainlink,** which provides decentralized price feeds and data services used by many DeFi platforms. **Pyth Network** focuses on delivering fast, low-latency market data from institutional sources, which is critical for trading and liquidation events. **Band Protocol** helps share data across blockchains, acting as a messenger and allowing different networks to communicate and verify information with each other. These oracle networks make decentralized applications more powerful, practical, and connected to the real world.

However, oracles also introduce risk. If an oracle is hacked, manipulated, or provides incorrect data, the smart contract will still execute based on that bad information.

This is why many platforms use multiple data sources and decentralized oracle networks instead of relying on a single provider.

AI and Blockchain: Different Tools for Different Problems

Artificial intelligence (AI) and blockchain are often discussed together, but they do very different jobs. Think of AI as a high-speed engine that looks at mountains of data to find patterns and make decisions. Blockchain, on the other hand, is like a permanent, digital record book that everyone trusts because it can't be changed.

In the crypto world, AI can act like a 24/7 security guard. It can scan thousands of transactions in a second to flag a scam or spot a hacker before they do any damage. While AI keeps an eye out for risks, blockchain provides the honest records that the AI needs to do its job accurately.

AI can also augment how humans interact with smart contracts. In practice, AI systems are being used to analyze smart contract behavior, monitor execution conditions, and suggest changes based on predefined rules and real-time data.

However, it's important to remember that AI is not a 'magic button.' It doesn't replace the need for human common sense or secure computer code. By keeping these two technologies separate conceptually, you can see where they help, preventing confusion and unrealistic expectations about what each technology can—and cannot—do.

Role Tokens and Altcoins Play in the Blockchain

"Tokens" are digital assets built on existing blockchains and are often part of an Initial Coin Offering (ICO) or Initial DEX Offering (IDO). There are different types of tokens in the cryptocurrency ecosystem, each serving a specific purpose.

Let us dive into the uses of tokens:

Tokens that function as digital money or a store of value are called **payment tokens**. **Utility tokens** allow access to a specific product or service within a blockchain ecosystem. **Security tokens** represent ownership of an asset (e.g., company shares, real estate). **Governance tokens** allow token owners to vote on protocol upgrades and changes. You can think of a cryptocurrency governance system as the local building property governance group, if your building was a blockchain.

Stablecoins are tied to the value of another currency (e.g. USD) to minimize volatility. **Non-Fungible Tokens (NFTs)** are unique digital assets used in gaming, art, and collectibles.

Wrapped tokens represent assets from another blockchain, created so that it can be used on a different chain that does not natively support them.

DeFi tokens power decentralized financial services like lending, trading, and staking. Below are examples of some of the most widely used tokens:

Payment Tokens (Cryptocurrencies)

- Bitcoin (BTC) – The first and most popular cryptocurrency.
- Litecoin (LTC) – A faster, lightweight version of Bitcoin.
- Bitcoin Cash (BCH) – A fork of Bitcoin with lower fees and faster transactions.
- Monero (XMR) – A privacy-focused cryptocurrency.

Utility Tokens

- Ethereum (ETH) – used for gas fees on the Ethereum blockchain and smart contract execution.
- Binance Coin (BNB) – used for transaction discounts on Binance and paying gas fees on the BNB Chain.
- Chainlink (LINK) – powers decentralized Oracle services.
- Filecoin (FIL) – used for decentralized storage services.

Security Tokens

- tZERO (TZROP) – a security token representing ownership in the tZERO platform.

- INX Token (INX) – represents ownership in the INX trading platform.
- Securitize (DS Protocol Tokens) – used for tokenized securities on the blockchain.

Governance Tokens

- Uniswap (UNI) – governance token for the Uniswap decentralized exchange.
- Maker (MKR) – used for governance in the MakerDAO ecosystem.
- Aave (AAVE) – allows voting on Aave lending platform policies.
- Compound (COMP) – used for governance in the Compound DeFi platform.

Stablecoins

- Tether (USDT) – pegged to the U.S. dollar, widely used in trading.
- USD Coin (USDC) – a stablecoin backed by reserves.
- DAI – a decentralized, collateral-backed stablecoin.
- Binance USD (BUSD) – another USD-backed stablecoin.

Non-Fungible Tokens (NFTs)

- Bored Ape Yacht Club (BAYC) – a famous NFT collection.
- CryptoPunks – one of the first NFT collections on Ethereum.
- Decentraland (MANA) – a token for virtual real estate in the Decentraland metaverse.

- Axie Infinity (AXS) – used in the Axie Infinity play-to-earn game.

DeFi (Decentralized Finance) Tokens

- Yearn Finance (YFI) – Used for automated yield farming.
- SushiSwap (SUSHI) – Governance token for the SushiSwap DEX.
- PancakeSwap (CAKE) – Used for governance and staking on the PancakeSwap DEX.
- Curve (CRV) – Powers the Curve Finance platform for stablecoin trading.

Wrapped Tokens

- Wrapped Bitcoin (WBTC) – This token is backed by Bitcoin on the Ethereum network.
- Wrapped Ether (WETH) – This is a wrapped version of ETH for DeFi applications.
- renBTC (renBTC) – This is a wrapped Bitcoin used on Ethereum and other blockchains.

Takeaway: Tokens are the foundation of the cryptocurrency ecosystem, each playing a crucial role in different blockchain applications.

The Role of Altcoins

"Altcoins" or alternate coins are any cryptocurrencies other than Bitcoin, such as Ethereum, Cardano, and Litecoin. These digital assets were developed to improve Bitcoin's limitations or serve specific use cases in the blockchain ecosystem. Altcoins offer faster transactions (e.g., Litecoin vs. Bitcoin), enable smart contracts (e.g., Ethereum, Solana), provide decentralized financial services (e.g., DeFi projects), and enhance security and privacy.

Below are examples of the widely used altcoins:

- Utility Tokens – used within a specific ecosystem, e.g. Ethereum (ETH), Chainlink (LINK).
- Stablecoins – are tied to a stable asset, such as USD (e.g., USDT, USDC, DAI).
- Security Tokens – represent asset ownership (e.g., INX Token, tZERO).
- Meme Coins – based on internet culture, meme coins are often speculative (e.g., Dogecoin (DOGE), Shiba Inu (SHIB)).

- DeFi Tokens – used in Decentralized Finance platforms (e.g. Uniswap (UNI), Aave (AAVE)).
- Privacy Coins – focus on anonymity (e.g., Monero (XMR), Zcash (ZEC)).

Can a token also be an altcoin? Yes! A token can be an altcoin, but not all altcoins are tokens.

How?

An altcoin is any cryptocurrency that is not Bitcoin
A token is a digital asset and part of a blockchain, like Ethereum, Solana, or Binance Smart Chain. Since tokens are part of the broader cryptocurrency ecosystem, they fall under the category of altcoin.

Tokens and altcoins are part of the cryptocurrency ecosystem and can represent various assets, including utility, governance, or collateral within a blockchain network. They may also be involved in DeFi platforms, NFT projects, or governance systems.

Takeaway: All tokens are altcoins, but not all altcoins are tokens—some are native coins.

Example Breakdown

Type	Example	Altcoin?	Token?
Coin (native blockchain)	Ethereum (ETH), Solana (SOL)	Yes	No
Utility Token	Chainlink (LINK), Uniswap (UNI)	Yes	Yes
Stablecoin	USDT (Tether), USDC	Yes	Yes
Security Token	tZERO (TZROP)	Yes	Yes

What Are Non-Fungible Tokens (NFTs)?

NFTs are unique digital assets that represent ownership of a physical or digital item. When an investor buys an NFT, they are not only purchasing the digital file (which can be copied); they are also acquiring the proof of ownership linked to the digital asset. For example, imagine a famous artist creates a piece of art and mints it as an NFT on the Ethereum blockchain. Anyone can view the art, but only the buyer holds verifiable ownership. Thus, an NFT functions much like owning the deed to a house or the title of a car. Blockchain networks verify the ownership and authenticity of NFTs. Unlike cryptocurrencies, which are interchangeable, NFTs represent unique items or content—such as art, music, in-game assets, or real estate—that can be sold or bought in the crypto market.

NFTs have gained significant attention, but the market has also faced scandals related to fraud, market manipulation, and copyright issues. For example, the Frosties NFT project in 2022 raised $1.3 million before its creators disappeared with the funds. These incidents undermine trust in the NFT market, especially for those without trading experience. They also raise ethical concerns about influencers taking advantage of less informed buyers.

NFTs typically reside on smart contract networks, such as Ethereum and Solana. They enhance the cryptocurrency ecosystem offerings.

Owning NFTs can introduce significant risks, including volatility and potential loss of investment. Examples of NFT-based ecosystems include Audius, a digital streaming music platform, and Decentraland, a 3D virtual reality space where users can explore, connect, buy, sell, and develop virtual land plots.

Takeaway: The NFT market has recently faced several scandals. Such issues increase public skepticism and call for more regulation within the crypto market. As the market matures, better mechanisms for authenticity verification, sustainable practices, and consumer protection will likely become more important to help reduce these issues and protect investors.

How Are Regulators Impacting Cryptocurrency Given the Risk Introduced by Decentralization?

Regulations directly impact the cryptocurrency ecosystem and the participation of its stakeholders. While they add a layer of consumer protection and security, they have a direct impact on how crypto projects are developed, traded, and adopted by the public.

Some territories, like the U.S., the European Union, and Japan, have introduced legal frameworks for cryptocurrencies that impact the market. In 2025, regulators focused on crypto consumer protection, Anti-Money Laundering (AML), and Data Privacy guidelines.

Regulators will continue to pressure crypto companies and financial institutions to implement applicable frameworks to protect consumer data, make practices more transparent, conduct regular compliance audits, and educate their employees. Regulators are pushing the crypto market toward greater legitimacy and increased integration with traditional financial markets, but the balance between innovation and control remains a topic that warrants further exploration.

Regulation creates safer, more trustworthy environments that attract more institutional investors. However, overregulation and unclear rules can hinder innovation and discourage open-source development.

There is a heightened level of oversight and compliance requirements related to Know Your Customer (KYC) and Anti-Money Laundering (AML) regulations. Crypto platforms must register with financial authorities or face the possibility of being excluded from certain markets (i.e., countries). These requirements are prompting many DeFi projects to explore compliance frameworks as the landscape continues to evolve.

Takeaway: Regulation plays a growing role in shaping the cryptocurrency ecosystem. Clear rules can improve consumer protection, increase trust, and encourage broader adoption—especially among institutions. At the same time, overly restrictive or unclear regulations can slow innovation and limit open-source development. Understanding this balance helps explain why regulation remains one of the most important—and debated—forces influencing the future of crypto.

What Are Crypto Wallets?

You may have heard the term "crypto wallet." A crypto wallet is software or hardware that allows users to **store, receive, and send cryptocurrencies** by managing the **private keys** needed to access digital assets on a blockchain and approve transactions. It is worth noting that crypto wallets do not store cryptocurrencies themselves; rather, they store the private keys that prove ownership and enable control over assets recorded on the blockchain.

There are two primary types of crypto wallets: **hot wallets** and **cold wallets**.

Hot wallets are connected to the internet and are typically software-based, including web, desktop, or mobile applications. They are easy to set up and convenient to use, making them well suited for everyday transactions and trading. However, because they are online, hot wallets are generally more vulnerable to hacking, phishing attacks, and malware.

Cold wallets store private keys offline, significantly reducing exposure to online threats. These wallets are commonly hardware devices, such as USB-like tools, designed specifically for secure key storage. Cold storage can also include paper wallets; however, paper wallets are now considered risky due to their susceptibility to loss, damage, or improper generation and are generally discouraged in favor of modern hardware wallets.

Individuals and businesses use different types of wallets depending on their needs, such as security, accessibility, and ease of use. These factors should be carefully considered when selecting a wallet.

Users who prioritize security—particularly for long-term or large holdings—often choose hardware wallets (cold wallets). Popular examples include the **Ledger Nano X** and **Trezor Model T**. Users who prioritize convenience and frequent access typically opt for **hot wallets**, such as *MetaMask, Trust Wallet, Exodus,* or *Coinbase Wallet,* which support multiple cryptocurrencies and are widely used.

Because the crypto ecosystem evolves rapidly, it is recommended that users conduct research before selecting a wallet, as new tools and security practices continue to emerge.

Common Wallet Categories

In addition to hot and cold storage, wallets can be grouped into several functional categories:

Web Wallets

Web wallets are accessed through a browser and are hosted by a service provider or operate through web-based interfaces. They are convenient and beginner-friendly but are generally less secure than hardware wallets because private keys may be exposed to online threats. Examples include **MyEtherWallet** and web-based blockchain explorers with wallet functionality.

Mobile Wallets

Mobile wallets are smartphone applications designed for quick access and everyday use. They often include built-in security features such as biometric authentication. Popular examples include Trust Wallet and MetaMask Mobile. Some wallets are platform-specific, but most modern mobile wallets support multiple operating systems and assets.

Multi-Signature Wallets

Multi-signature (multisig) wallets require approval from multiple private keys to authorize a transaction, increasing security and reducing single points of failure. They are commonly used by organizations, investment groups, or individuals managing high-value assets. *BitGo* is a well-known provider of multisignature wallet solutions.

Custodial Wallets

Custodial wallets are managed by third-party providers, such as cryptocurrency exchanges, which hold and control users' private keys on their behalf. While these wallets are user-friendly and suitable for beginners, they require users to trust the provider with custody of their assets. **Coinbase** is a common example of a custodial wallet.

While some custodial platforms offer insurance protections, these typically apply only to **U.S. dollar balances**, not cryptocurrencies themselves. As a result, users do not have full control over their private keys, which introduces counterparty risk.

Takeaway: Wallets are not strictly required to trade cryptocurrencies, as many exchanges provide custodial wallets for users. However, they are strongly recommended. Wallets increase security and provide greater control. If an exchange is hacked and suspends withdrawals, users may lose access to their funds. With a wallet, you control the private keys and access to your funds directly.

How Do Private Keys and Seed Phrases Work?

A private key is a long secret code that gives users control over their cryptocurrency at a specific address on the blockchain. It can be compared to a password that unlocks a specific bank account. Private keys are used to "sign" transactions, which prove ownership of funds and authorize the blockchain to send them to other addresses.

A seed phrase, also referred to as a recovery key, is a set of 12-24 words that act as a master key to your entire crypto wallet. Your seed phrase is generated when you set up your crypto wallet. If you lose your device or wallet software, your seed phrase can be used to restore your wallet and gain access to your funds. A seed phrase can be compared to the "deed" to your house. In this example, the private key is the key to your house that gives you control and access to what's inside. However, if your house burns down or is destroyed, you can use the deed to the house (the seed phrase) to rebuild the house or regain control of your property.

Keep in mind that if someone gets your private key or "seed phrase," they can control your funds. Keep it secure, preferably offline! Losing your private keys means you cannot access your wallet, and there is no way to recover your funds unless you have a backup, such as a recovery seed phrase.

You need a private key to access cold and hot wallets, but how you use it depends on the type of wallet. Modern cold wallets (e.g., *Ledger, Trezor*) use seed phrases that derive your private keys. Should you lose your device, you can restore your account using the seed phrase. However, if both your private key and seed phrase are lost, your crypto will be permanently inaccessible.

The diagram below illustrates a simple Bitcoin exchange between Daniel and Amelia. Daniel is using a hot wallet on his mobile device, and Amelia is receiving BTC and storing it in her cold wallet (physical device) using her private key.

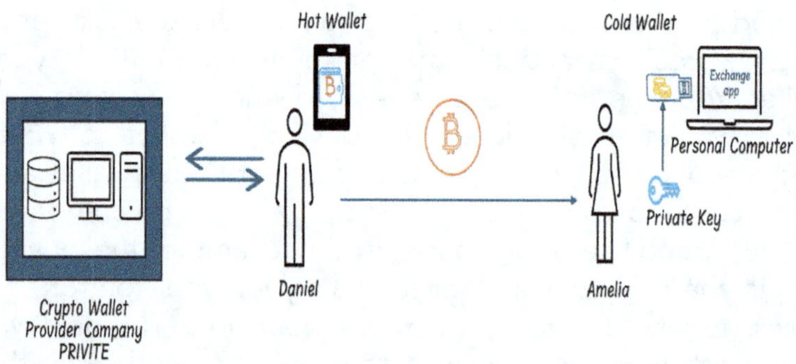

Security Tip: Storing your private key online is risky and not safe for substantial crypto holdings. Keep them offline! Write down your seed phrase and keep a physical backup in a secure place. Remember, if you lose your private key and seed phrase, your crypto will be lost forever!

What Drives Cryptocurrency Prices?

Cryptocurrency prices are driven by several factors, including supply and demand, inflation, economic conditions, investor sentiment, and market news. A limited supply (like Bitcoin's 21 million coins cap) and rising demand drive prices upward. Positive events such as institutional adoption or technology upgrades increase optimism and prices. Negative news, like regulatory crackdowns, can lower prices.

FOMO (Fear Of Missing Out) occurs when rising prices and market optimism lead investors to buy assets quickly, often out of a fear that they are being left behind by a growing trend.

Panic selling during fear and uncertainty causes downturns, but innovation (like network upgrades or new apps) attracts investors. However, it isn't just technology or data that moves the needle; the power of public opinion is equally influential.

Media and social influencers can quickly shift prices; celebrity commentary can exacerbate crypto price swings and draw regulatory attention.

Can a single individual manipulate the crypto market? Influential people can have a significant impact on the crypto market, either positively or negatively, simply by commenting on social media, thereby increasing volatility and investor risk.

An idea, behavior, or piece of media that spreads rapidly and is often altered or imitated across social media and the internet is called a "Meme." Dogecoin is an example of a meme cryptocurrency. The term meme was initially introduced by Richard Dawkins, an English evolutionary biologist, in 1976. He authored the book "The Selfish Gene," in which he introduced the term "meme" to describe how cultural information spreads, much like the transmission of genes. Fast-forward to 2025, memes are primarily associated with the internet or social media culture and are used to convey jokes, trends, or commentary.

Beginners should identify trusted sources of information, such as well-established publications and reputable news outlets, to make informed decisions and lower their risk when navigating the crypto market. Changes in how cryptocurrencies are taxed can significantly influence the behavior of the cryptocurrency market.

Clear and favorable regulations often boost prices by attracting institutional investors. However, rising interest rates can make crypto assets less attractive, given their speculative nature.

Market size matters: smaller cryptocurrencies are more prone to extreme price swings due to their lower market capitalization, which is defined as the total value of a company's outstanding shares of stock units multiplied by the number of shares in circulation.

Formula:

In the cryptocurrency market, market capitalization (market cap) refers to the total value of all coins of a cryptocurrency that are currently in circulation. It is calculated by multiplying the current price per coin by the total number of coins in circulation.

Market Cap = Current Price per Coin X Total Circulating Supply

For example, if cryptocurrency X has 10 million coins in circulation and the price of each coin is $50, then its market capitalization is $500 million.

Market cap helps compare the size and stability of different cryptocurrencies. A larger market capitalization usually indicates that the coin is more stable and less risky, while a smaller market capitalization means the coin may be more volatile. Generally, large-cap cryptocurrencies (those with a market capitalization of over $10 billion, such as Bitcoin or Ethereum) are considered more stable and lower risk.

Mid-cap cryptocurrencies ($1B - $10B) offer moderate risk and growth potential, while small-cap cryptocurrencies (under $1B) are higher risk but have greater potential for reward.

The figure below illustrates key factors that drive cryptocurrency prices up or down.

What is Tokenomics and How Does it Impact the Crypto Market?

Tokenomics is the study of economic factors that influence a crypto token or digital asset, as well as how they are managed. It analyzes the total number of tokens in circulation and how new tokens are created and allocated. It also determines what tokens are used for, how tokens are protected, how the value of the token changes over time, and how incentives are created. Tokenomics helps people compare different cryptocurrencies and make informed decisions. Imagine buying a car and reviewing the facts before making a purchase.

With this background in mind, let's examine the specific tokenomics of the two leading cryptocurrencies:

BTC's Tokenomics: Main and most valuable coin.
- Bitcoin's supply cap is 21 million coins.
- New Bitcoins are released through a reward system for miners.
- The limited number of Bitcoins circulating is a primary driver for its price.

ETH's Tokenomics: The native currency used to pay for transaction fees and participate in staking.

- Proof of Stake has reduced ETH issuance and introduced staking rewards to validators.
- Ethereum supports various ERC-20[2] tokens, serving different purposes in the ecosystem.
- The evolving supply model of ETH, particularly with staking and transaction fee burning, positions ETH as potentially scarce and more valuable over time if demand for the network continues to grow.

Tip: The cryptocurrency market is heavily influenced by speculation, and it can be unpredictable; therefore, individuals investing in the crypto market should not invest more money than they can afford to lose. Individual investors often trade against highly sophisticated players, and that does not make it easy for beginners.

---

[2]"ERC-20" stands for "Ethereum Request for Comments 20," which defines the rules for creating interoperable tokens on the Ethereum blockchain. For more details, see Ethereum Foundation, ERC-20 Token Standard.
https://ethereum.org/en/developers/docs/standards/tokens/erc-20

Chapter 3

Which Cryptocurrencies Are Most Widely Used?

According to data from Tangem and CoinMarketCap.com, a staggering 25,000 cryptocurrencies existed as of February 2025. This number reflects the rapid changes within the blockchain and cryptocurrency industry. Still, many of these tokens may be inactive or lack substantial value. It will be impossible to be familiar with all cryptocurrencies. This chapter focuses on the most widely known cryptocurrencies based on the market as of February 2025.

Remember, investing in cryptocurrencies carries inherent risks due to market volatility. Digital asset investors should conduct thorough research and carefully assess the risk they are willing to tolerate before making investment decisions.

The U.S. Securities Exchange Commission (SEC) defines risk tolerance as "an investor's ability and willingness to lose some or all of an investment in exchange for greater potential returns."

Overview of Bitcoin (BTC), Ethereum (ETH), and Other Major Coins

Bitcoin is highly popular, but it is not the only cryptocurrency in the market. There are plenty of options for those who cannot afford the BTC price. The exact number of cryptocurrencies changes frequently as new ones are created, and others are abandoned or fail.

New coins or tokens are frequently created using Initial Coin Offerings (ICOs), Initial DEX Offerings (IDOs), or token launches. Those could be new blockchains, like Avalanche or Polkadot, or tokens built on existing blockchains, like ERC-20 on Ethereum.

In 2025 there were a few dominant cryptocurrencies, including Bitcoin (BTC), Ethereum (ETH), Binance Coin (BNB), Cardano (ADA), Solana (SOL), XRP (XRP), Polkadot (DOT), SUI, LINK, LEO and Tether (USDT). These are among the top cryptocurrencies by market capitalization (as of May 2025) according to CoinMarketCap.[3]

---

[3] "CoinMarketCap" is a cryptocurrency data aggregator that provides real-time market data. Data was as of May 7, 2025. https://coinmarketcap.com/

Bitcoin (BTC)

Bitcoin is the first cryptocurrency, a medium of exchange that exists exclusively online. Bitcoin is a decentralized digital currency that enables peer-to-peer online transactions without the need for a central authority, such as a bank or government.

Ethereum (ETH)

Ethereum is the second most widely recognized coin and token after BTC. The Ethereum network can be used as currency and it performs several functions, including supporting smart contracts, contributing to its popularity.

Tether (USDT)

Tether functions as a pivotal stablecoin within the cryptocurrency ecosystem, primarily by facilitating trade and ensuring essential market liquidity.

However, its backing has been a source of notable concern; skeptics worry that Tether's reserves are not fully secured by U.S. dollars. Instead, the coin is known to utilize a portfolio that includes short-term, unsecured commercial debt. Tether can move between blockchains, and it allows for swaps, provides redemption for fiat currency and insurance.

USD Coin (USDC)

USDC is a fiat-backed stablecoin that is designed to maintain a stable value. Like Tether, USD coin is a stablecoin linked to the U.S. dollar, meaning its value should not fluctuate. The value of a USDC coin is pegged to the value of the dollar and backed by reserve assets for price stability.

XRP (XRP)

XRP is the native cryptocurrency of the XRP Ledger (XRPL), an open-source, decentralized ledger technology. Its main purpose is to serve as a "bridge currency" in cross-border payments. XRP allows financial institutions to send money internationally almost instantly and with very low fees.

BNB (BNB)

BNB is the native token[4] of the entire BNB Chain ecosystem and one of the largest cryptocurrencies by market capitalization. BNB (originally "Binance Coin," now standing for "Build and Build") is the utility token that powers the entire BNB Chain ecosystem. It was launched in 2017 by the cryptocurrency exchange, Binance (globally recognized) and it is used to pay for discounted trades and purchase various goods and services.

Solana (SOL)

Solana is a public, open-source (publicly available code) blockchain platform designed to host highly scalable decentralized applications (dApps), often serving as a direct competitor to Ethereum due to its focus on speed, low cost, and high throughput. The project was founded by Anatoly Yakovenko and was officially launched in March 2020 by Solana Labs.

---

[4] "Native token" refers to the primary digital asset inherently issued by a blockchain network, used for transactions, paying network fees, incentivizing validators/miners, and supporting network security and governance. https://www.coinapi.io/learn/glossary/native-toke

Dogecoin (DOGE)

Dogecoin was created as a joke after the run-up in Bitcoin; Dogecoin inherited the name from an online meme about a Shiba Inu dog. Unlike many digital currencies limiting the number of coins, Dogecoin has unlimited issuance. It is used to make payments and send money. It was initially created to make fun of the cryptocurrency industry and raise awareness of blockchain technology.

Cardano (ADA)

Cardano is an open-source, decentralized public blockchain platform known for its rigorous, academic-driven development approach.
Launched in 2017, the platform is designed to be a third-generation blockchain, aiming to address the scalability, interoperability, and sustainability issues inherent in earlier technologies like Bitcoin and Ethereum. Cardano supports smart contracts for identity management.

TRON (TRX)

TRON is a decentralized, open-source blockchain platform that aims to decentralize the internet by building infrastructure for a global, free digital content entertainment system. Its main goal is to eliminate middlemen (like YouTube or Google Play) between content creators and consumers, allowing creators to share and monetize their work directly. The native utility cryptocurrency of the TRON blockchain is called TRONix, or TRX. It is used as the primary method of payment and exchange for services and digital content within the TRON ecosystem.

Avalanche (AVAX)

Avalanche, launched in 2020, is a crypto known for its high transaction speeds and low costs. The Avalanche blockchain is also notable for creating subnets, which are custom blockchains with their own rules and use cases, allowing developers to meet different technological needs as they see fit.

Sui (SUI)

Sui is a Layer 1[5] blockchain and smart contract platform designed for high scalability, low latency (fast transaction speed), and near-instant finality. It is often highlighted as a competitor to other high-throughput Layer 1 networks like Solana. Sui was created by former Meta engineers to enable fast transactions while charging stable fees. It can handle many transactions simultaneously, making it scalable.

LINK

The LINK token is an ERC-677 token (an extension of the ERC-20 standard on the Ethereum blockchain) that serves as the economic engine and primary means of value transfer within the Chainlink ecosystem.

---

[5]"Layer 1 (L1)" refers to the foundational blockchain architecture where all transactions are validated and recorded. It defines the network's consensus, security, and governance. https://koinly.io/crypto-glossary/layer-1-blockchain/

Chainlink is not a typical blockchain; it is a Decentralized Oracle Network (DON). Its core function is to solve the "oracle problem," which is the inability of blockchain smart contracts to access data from the outside world (off-chain) in a secure, reliable, and tamper-proof way.

UNUS SED LEO (LEO)

UNUS SED LEO (LEO), is the exchange utility token of the iFinex ecosystem, the parent company of the cryptocurrency exchange, Bitfinex. LEO was primarily designed to provide tangible benefits and cost savings for users within the iFinex family of products, mainly in the Bitfinex exchange. LEO owners aim to gradually reduce its supply to zero by buying back LEO tokens from the open market and permanently removing them from circulation (burn them).

Author Disclaimer: Investors should conduct independent research into investment strategies before making an investment decision. Past investment product performance does not guarantee future price increases.

Differences Between Stablecoins, Utility Tokens, and Meme Coins

There are three categories of cryptocurrencies: stablecoins, utility tokens, and meme coins. Each refers to a different type of cryptocurrency with unique purposes and characteristics.

Stablecoins provide stability and are primarily used as a medium of exchange or store of value within the crypto ecosystem. They maintain a stable value by being pegged to an external asset, typically a fiat currency (e.g., the U.S. Dollar) or a basket of assets (e.g., commodities like gold). Their primary goal is to reduce volatility, making them more suitable for daily transactions and as a store of value compared to traditional cryptocurrencies like Bitcoin or Ethereum.

Stablecoins can be used in the following ways:

- Collateral protection against volatility in the crypto market.

- Facilitating trading and transferring value between exchanges without converting to fiat currency.

- DeFi applications, where stablecoins are used for lending, borrowing, and earning interest.

A **utility token** is a type of cryptocurrency designed to perform a specific function inside a digital platform or blockchain network. Instead of being used only for speculation, utility tokens act like **digital access keys** — they allow users to use services, pay for actions, or unlock features within a system.

For example, **Ether (ETH)** is used to pay transaction fees (called gas fees) on the Ethereum network. **BNB** is used to reduce trading fees on Binance and to pay for transactions on the BNB Chain. MATIC (Polygon) is used to run applications and process transactions on the Polygon network. In these cases, the token is required for the platform to function — without it, the network can't operate.

Utility tokens are also used in gaming, where players spend tokens to buy in-game items, land, or upgrades, and in **DeFi platforms**, where tokens are needed to borrow, lend, vote on upgrades, or earn rewards.

Some platforms even use utility tokens as membership passes that give users voting rights or discounts.

Because utility tokens are tied to how useful and popular a platform becomes, their prices can rise or fall significantly. If a project grows and more people use it, demand for the token increases. If adoption slows, the token's value may drop. This makes utility tokens more volatile than stablecoins, but generally more grounded in real usage than meme coins.

Meme coins are cryptocurrencies that gain popularity mainly through social media, internet culture, and online communities rather than real-world utility. Their value is often driven by hype, celebrity mentions, viral trends, or jokes that spread quickly online. Unlike utility tokens, meme coins usually have **little practical use** beyond entertainment and community engagement.

Because meme coins are driven by speculation, their prices can rise and fall extremely fast. A single tweet or viral post can cause prices to surge, while loss of attention can make them crash just as quickly. This makes meme coins **high-risk investments**, especially for beginners who may not understand how quickly momentum can disappear.

Meme coins are sometimes used in **pump-and-dump schemes**, where a small group of people hype the coin, drive the price up, and then sell, leaving others with heavy losses. Still, meme coins can also have positive community moments. For example, Dogecoin has been used for charitable fundraising, including helping sponsor the Jamaican bobsled team.

For many investors, meme coins are less like traditional investments and more like digital collectibles or lottery tickets — fun to watch, but risky to rely on.

Takeaway: Stablecoins, utility tokens, and meme coins serve very different purposes in the crypto world.

Stablecoins are designed to stay close to the value of traditional money and are used for payments, saving, and trading stability.

Utility tokens are used to power platforms and unlock real services, so their value depends on how useful and popular a network becomes. Meme coins are driven by hype and community excitement, making them highly volatile and speculative.

For beginners, understanding the difference is key: stablecoins are tools, utility tokens are fuel, and meme coins are hype — and each comes with its own level of risk.

Coins Key Differences

Aspect	Stablecoins	Utility Tokens	Meme Coins
Purpose	Maintain a stable value, usually pegged to fiat currencies	Access services or features on a blockchain platform	Primarily for fun, community engagement, or speculation
Value Stability	Stable, pegged to a fiat currency or asset	Can be volatile, tied to the success of the platform	Highly volatile, often driven by memes or trends
Examples	Tether (USDT), USD Coin (USDC), DAI	Ethereum (ETH), Chainlink (LINK), Uniswap (UNI)	Dogecoin (DOGE), Shiba Inu (SHIB)
Use Cases	Hedging, trading, transferring value, DeFi	Pay for services, governance, platform access	Speculation, community engagement, fun
Market Behavior	Low volatility, often tied to fiat currency	Can fluctuate based on platform success and demand	Highly speculative, subject to social trends and hype

What Are NFTs and How Are They Used?

Non-Fungible Tokens (NFTs) are distinctive digital assets stored on a blockchain. They primarily represent ownership or proof of authenticity for various items, which can include art, collectibles, music, and even virtual real estate. NFTs are also used to code smart contract rules, and they function as gaming assets that players own and trade.

However, NFTs also carry significant risks. They have often been instruments of speculation, scams, and fraud. In many cases, these assets are not traded for a specific use but are bought and sold primarily for profit. NFTs are typically traded on specialized blockchain marketplaces, such as OpenSea, Blur, Rarible, Magic Eden, and Foundation.

In 2021, the NFT market experienced explosive growth, surpassing $17 billion in trading volume. However, by late 2022, the market became oversaturated, and trading volume plummeted to less than $500 million.

This sharp decline was driven by price volatility, hype fatigue, copycat projects, scams, and low-quality offerings. The rise and fall of NFTs offer important lessons: true value lies in utility and long-term benefits, not just speculation. Brand credibility also plays a crucial role, and potential investors should thoroughly research creators and their ecosystems before making any purchases.

Before investing in NFTs, beginners should take time to thoroughly research and understand each project. Start small, stay cautious, and be aware of potential scams. Focus on projects that demonstrate real utility and transparent goals. Understand all associated fees, track your investments, and approach NFTs as long-term assets rather than quick-profit opportunities. Always use a trusted crypto wallet, securely record your recovery phrase, and store it offline. Tools such as DappRadar, NFTBank, and Zapper can help you monitor your portfolio and assess performance over time.

Below are some notable examples of NFTs:

Digital Art

CryptoPunks is a form of digital art and one of the first NFT projects on the Ethereum blockchain. It consists of 10,000 pixelated characters, each with unique features. Some have sold for millions of dollars, and these characters have become iconic in the NFT space.

"Bored Ape Yacht Club" (BAYC) is a collection of 10,000 unique, hand-drawn ape avatars. Each NFT in the collection comes with membership to an exclusive community, which includes events and access to additional digital content.

Beeple's "Everyday: The First 5000 Days" is a digital artwork created by artist Mike Winkelmann, known as Beeple. He created a collage of 5,000 digital images daily over 13 years. The artwork was sold as an NFT at a historic Christie's auction in March 2021 for an astounding $69.3 million, making it one of the most expensive digital art pieces sold in history.

This sale marked a significant moment in the NFT and digital art world, showcasing the growing value of blockchain-based assets. You might wonder what one would do with such a piece of art.

This NFT is a unique, verifiable proof of ownership recorded on the blockchain, making it a potential long-term investment. The artwork can be showcased in virtual galleries, metaverse spaces, or even projected in physical exhibitions. Some buyers of NFTs display them on digital screens in their homes or offices. It could also be used for future commercial purposes like licensing deals, digital content, or collaborations in various industries, such as gaming, media, and virtual reality. The purchase was likely an investment in digital art and a symbolic move to support NFTs.

Collectibles

CryptoKitties is one of the first blockchain-based games. This game lets users buy, sell, and breed digital cats (digital creatures). Each cat is a unique NFT with various traits and features. These digital crypto collectibles have played a pivotal role in the evolution of blockchain-based assets.

CryptoKitties was launched in late 2017 on the Ethereum blockchain and invented by Canadian studio Axiom Zen. The game was an immediate hit, becoming very popular and generating more than $5 million in transactions after a week. This traffic led to network congestion and slowness on the Ethereum network. These challenges brought attention to the potential and scalability of blockchain technology. In 2019, the game moved to the Flow blockchain (a next-generation platform), making it more scalable. Flow is a proof-of-stake blockchain designed for Web3, a next-generation version of the internet, and for supporting the open metaverse. It enables applications such as NFTs, DeFi, DAOs, and profile picture (PFP) projects.

Virtual Real Estate

Decentraland is a 3D (three-dimensional) virtual reality environment where users buy, sell, and develop parcels of virtual land as NFTs. These virtual plots can create virtual experiences, such as gaming, shopping, or art galleries. Founded by Argentine developers Esteban Ordano and Ari Meilich, the project began as a proof of concept in 2015.

Music and Media

Audius is a decentralized music streaming platform where artists can release their music as NFTs. This platform offers artists more control over their music rights and profits, as well as more revenue control and new opportunities for musicians.

The history of music and media NFTs is closely linked to the evolution of blockchain technology and the emergence of digital ownership. In March 2021, the American rock band Kings of Leon released an NFT album titled "When You See Yourself." This release marked a milestone in music distribution, transforming traditional ownership models and redefining fan engagement.

The project generated approximately $2 million in sales, with a portion of the proceeds donated to the Live Nation and Crew Nation Global Relief Fund to support live music crews affected by the COVID-19 pandemic.

How Is Decentralized Finance (DeFi) Used?

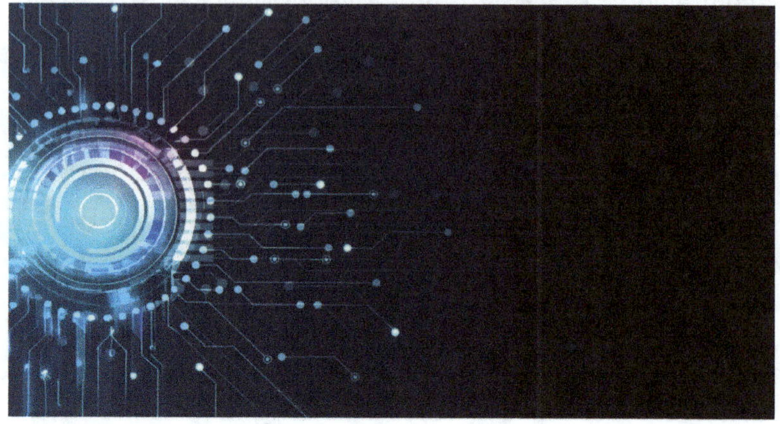

DeFi offers diverse financial services and products designed for blockchain technology. DeFi allows users to obtain financial services without intermediaries like central banks. Here are some examples of DeFi platforms:

Decentralized Exchanges (DEXs)

Uniswap is an open-source (open for public use) decentralized exchange (DEX) that uses smart contracts on the Ethereum blockchain. It enables trades between users, allowing them to swap tokens using their wallets.

Uniswap operates using an Automated Market Maker (AMM) model, in which users—known as liquidity providers—supply tokens to trading pools and earn a portion of the transaction fees in return. According to the Corporate Finance Institute (CFI), "**Liquidity** in cryptocurrency refers to the ease with which a digital token can be converted into another asset or cash without significantly affecting its price." In this model, liquidity pools depend on users to fund them, and aid efficient trading and market stability.

SushiSwap like *Uniswap* is a decentralized exchange and *AMM platform* that allows users to swap, stake, and earn rewards. Although it was created as a Uniswap fork, it has unique features and tokenomics. SushiSwap, like Uniswap, is a decentralized exchange (DEX) and automated market maker (AMM) that enables users to swap, stake, and earn rewards. Although it originated as a fork of Uniswap, SushiSwap introduced several innovations that distinguish it from its predecessor.

One of its main differentiators is the SUSHI token, which not only rewards liquidity providers but also grants governance rights, allowing holders to participate in protocol decisions. *SushiSwap* also offers yield farming[6] and staking opportunities through the SushiBar (xSUSHI), and additional products such as Kashi (a lending and margin trading platform) and BentoBox, a flexible vault system for DeFi applications. These features, combined with a community-driven approach and sustainable reward mechanisms, give SushiSwap a broader ecosystem and more complex tokenomics than traditional AMMs.

---

[6]"Farming (Yield Farming)" involves lending or staking cryptocurrency in exchange for interest or other rewards. It allows investors to earn passive income by providing liquidity to DeFi protocols. https://coinmarketcap.com/academy/article/what-is-yield-farming

Lending and Borrowing Platforms

Cryptocurrency lending and borrowing platforms allow users to lend, borrow, and earn interest on digital assets, often by using crypto holdings as collateral. These platforms fall into two main categories: Centralized Finance (CeFi) and Decentralized Finance (DeFi).

CeFi lending platforms are operated by centralized companies that manage user funds, set interest rates, and approve loans, functioning similarly to traditional financial institutions but focused on digital assets. DeFi platforms, by contrast, rely on blockchain-based smart contracts to automate lending and borrowing, enabling peer-to-peer transactions without intermediaries and offering greater transparency and user autonomy.

Examples of CeFi lending platforms in 2025 include *Nexo*, *Binance*, *Ledn*, *Arch*, and *CoinRabbit*. Prominent DeFi platforms include *Aave*, *Compound*, *MakerDAO*, and *Venus Protocol*.

While each platform operates differently, all aim to facilitate crypto lending and borrowing through distinct governance, risk management, and operational models.

CoinRabbit (CeFi) is a centralized crypto lending platform that allows users to borrow funds by posting cryptocurrency—such as Bitcoin or Ethereum—as collateral. Loans are typically issued in stablecoins like USDT or USDC and are governed by predefined loan-to-value (LTV) ratios. The platform actively monitors collateral and may liquidate assets if values fall below required thresholds. While *CoinRabbit* offers flexible repayment terms and minimal verification, users must trust the platform's risk controls, custody practices, and regulatory posture.

Aave (DeFi) is an open-source liquidity protocol built on the Ethereum blockchain that enables users to lend and borrow assets through smart contracts. By removing intermediaries, *Aave* allows users to interact directly with the protocol while maintaining transparency on-chain. Its innovations have played a significant role in shaping modern decentralized lending markets.

Compound (DeFi) is another decentralized lending protocol that allows users to supply and borrow crypto assets using algorithmically determined interest rates. Governance decisions are made by token holders, demonstrating how decentralized systems can manage credit markets without centralized control.

The fundamental distinction between CeFi and DeFi lending lies in trust, control, and risk allocation. CeFi platforms offer convenience, customer support, and in some cases regulatory oversight, but require users to relinquish control of their assets.

DeFi platforms provide greater transparency and user control through smart contracts, but introduce risks such as smart contract vulnerabilities, protocol failures, and market volatility. Understanding these trade-offs helps users determine which model best aligns with their risk tolerance and investment goals.

Tip: Compare interest rates, loan-to-value ratios, and repayment terms across lending platforms to find the best fit for you. Compare at least three lending platforms.

Yield Farming and Staking

In simple terms, **yield** is the interest or profit your investment generates over time. In the crypto world, this usually happens in two ways:

Yield Farming functions much the same as renting out a property. Just as a landlord provides space for a tenant and collects monthly rent, you provide your cryptocurrency to a platform to help it operate. In exchange for "renting" your assets to the platform, you receive a portion of the transaction fees. For example, providing $100 worth of Ethereum to a decentralized exchange might result in a 5% return in additional crypto over the year.

Staking, on the other hand, serves as a digital security deposit. It is comparable to a Certificate of Deposit (CD) at a traditional bank.

You agree to lock your tokens into the network to help verify transactions and maintain security. Because you are helping the "digital bank" run smoothly, the network pays you a "thank you" fee in the form of extra tokens. If you stake 100 tokens, you might find 105 in your wallet a year later as a reward for your loyalty and service to the network.

Yearn.finance (YFI) is a DeFi yield aggregator that automatically moves users' assets across various lending protocols (like Aave or Compound) to maximize returns. Users can deposit assets into Yearn's vaults to earn interest or use yield farming strategies. The platform optimizes yield generation for users by aggregating and managing lending and trading opportunities across different DeFi protocols to maximize returns for users.

"Curve Finance" is a decentralized exchange (DEX) optimized for stablecoin trading. It allows users to earn fees by providing liquidity to stablecoin pools. It offers yield farming opportunities with its native *CRV (Curve DAO Token)* token, a utility and governance token that can participate in Curve DAO (decentralized Autonomous Organization) governance, voting, fees structures, and liquidity incentives.

Takeaway: Crypto yield allows you to earn returns by using your digital assets to support networks or platforms. While yield farming and staking can generate additional income, they also carry risks tied to market conditions, platform security, and smart contracts. Always understand how returns are earned before participating.

Risks Associated with Lending and Borrowing Platforms

Investors and borrowers should understand the risks associated with lending and borrowing cryptocurrencies.

The primary risks include:

1. Market volatility could cause a drop in collateral value that can lead to liquidation.
2. Smart contracts come with their own risk as protocols can be exploited or hacked.
3. Regulatory uncertainty around CeFi platforms can face legal challenges from regulators.
4. **Custodial risk** with CeFi–the possibility of losing access to your funds as they are held by a third-party platform, who has direct control of your assets.

Some key risks can be mitigated by using reputable platforms and diversifying holdings so that not all holdings are stored on one platform. Investors can also reduce their risk by withdrawing profits frequently and regularly checking the platform revenues to see that they can cover their financial liabilities. Some platforms publish proof of earnings demonstrating that they hold enough assets to cover liabilities.

Stablecoins

Stablecoins are cryptocurrencies whose value is pegged to a fiat currency (e.g., the U.S. dollar) to maintain relative price stability. These assets typically live on public networks such as Ethereum or Tron, which allows anyone with a wallet to trade or redeem them for fiat currency at any time.

In the fast-moving world of crypto, stablecoins serve as the essential bridge between traditional finance and digital assets. Unlike Bitcoin, which can swing in value hourly, stablecoins are designed to stay pegged to a steady asset. This creates a "safe harbor" where you can store value without leaving the blockchain. Because millions of users may rely on a stablecoin to move or store value, regulators focus on questions of **reserve quality, transparency, and cash conversion**, aiming to ensure that stablecoin issuers can meet obligations during periods of market stress.

Understanding these coins requires looking at where they live and how they are built. On one hand, we have **Public Stablecoins**, which are the "Main Street" of crypto. They are accessible to everyone and provide the transparency of an open ledger. On the other hand, we have **Private or Consortium Stablecoins**, which function more as "Walled Gardens." These are issued by organizations like JPMorgan for internal use among banks.

While public coins offer broad usability, these private versions focus on high-speed settling within a controlled, audited environment.

The two most popular public stablecoins, **USDC** and **DAI**, represent two very different philosophies of trust. **USDC** is a centralized stablecoin, issued by a regulated company and backed 1:1 by actual cash and government bonds held in traditional banks.

USDC is often described as the "corporate dollar" of the crypto world because it is issued and managed by a centralized company that holds traditional financial reserves. In contrast, DAI operates without a single issuing company and is governed through decentralized rules rather than a central office. To keep its value stable, DAI requires users to lock up more cryptocurrency than the value of the DAI they receive, creating a buffer that helps absorb market swings.

Navigating the Risks

Every bridge has its weak points, and stablecoins are no exception. When using centralized coins, you face Counterparty Risk, meaning you must trust that the issuing company and their partner banks hold the reserves they claim to have.

There is also regulatory risk, where a government could suddenly freeze certain accounts or change the rules on how these coins are issued. For decentralized coins, the threat is often smart contract risk, where a bug in the code could be exploited. Furthermore, algorithmic models face liquidation risk; if the value of the crypto used as collateral drops too sharply, the entire system can become unstable.

Whether it operates as a "walled garden" with centralized control or a "public square" open to all, the stability of a coin is only as strong as the transparency of its reserves and the security of the code that powers it.

How Stablecoins Support DeFi / Liquidity Pools?

The stability created by stablecoins is the foundation for Decentralized Finance (DeFi), specifically through a concept known as **Liquidity Pools**. While traditional markets require you to wait for a buyer to match your sell order, a Liquidity Pool functions as an **Automated Money Exchange Kiosk** that never closes. You and other users serve as "Liquidity Providers" by stocking this kiosk with a balanced pair of tokens—for instance, an equal value of Ethereum and USDC.

When you deposit your assets, you are providing the necessary inventory that enables others to trade instantly. This setup eliminates the need for a middleman or a waiting period. In exchange for keeping the kiosk stocked and ready for business, you earn a proportional share of the trading fees generated by every transaction that passes through the pool. You are effectively putting your crypto to work, providing a vital service to the network while collecting a fee for your contribution.

Example:

- Deposit 1 ETH ($1,000) and 1,000 USDC into a pool.

- Traders swap ETH/USDC from the pool instantly.

- The exchange charges a 0.3% fee per trade.

- You earn a share of that fee proportional to the liquidity you provide.

Popular platforms for liquidity provision include *Uniswap, Curve Finance, Balancer, PancakeSwap*, and *GMX*.

> *Risks: If the price fluctuates too much, you could end up with fewer tokens than you started with. If planforms are hacked, your funds could be at risk. If the pool is not used by many people, your rewards may be low.*

Crypto Insurance Protocols

The crypto market offers less widespread and less regulated insurance solutions than traditional financial insurance. While traditional banks and investment accounts often have government-backed protection—such as FDIC (Federal Deposit Insurance Corporation) or SIPC (Securities Investor Protection Corporation) insurance in the U.S.—crypto assets generally do not have automatic coverage. Cryptocurrency insurance is designed to protect against specific risks, including cybersecurity hacks, smart contract failures, exchange insolvency, loss of funds, and theft.

Decentralized Insurance Platforms

Platforms like *Nexus Mutual* and *Unslashed* allow users to purchase coverage for smart contract failures, hacks, and other crypto-specific risks. For example:

- Nexus Mutual enables users to buy insurance against smart contract vulnerabilities or exchange hacks by pooling risk among members.

- Unslashed provides coverage for custodial losses, Decentralized Finance (DeFi) protocol failures, and stablecoin de-pegging events (when a stablecoin's value deviates from its intended fiat peg).

Centralized / Commercial Insurance

Some centralized crypto platforms that hold assets on behalf of users (called custodians) offer limited insurance coverage.

This insurance may help in rare cases like a platform hack, but it usually does not cover losses caused by price drops, scams, or user errors.

Coinbase provides insurance coverage for digital assets stored in online wallets, covering theft due to hacks of their systems, but does not cover individual account breaches or losses due to user error.

BitGo offers insurance for assets stored in their custody solutions, generally up to hundreds of millions of dollars, but coverage limits, exclusions, and terms vary.

How Crypto Insurance Works vs. Traditional Insurance

Traditional insurance often protects against a broad set of events, regulated by government authorities, and comes with legal recourse.

Crypto insurance is more niche and voluntary, typically covering very specific risks like smart contract failure or exchange insolvency. It is often community-governed (in the case of decentralized platforms), and claims are processed according to the protocol's rules rather than legal mandates.

Limitations and Risks:

- Coverage is usually limited in amount and scope, meaning a catastrophic hack could exceed insured limits.

- Decentralized insurance protocols are themselves exposed to smart contract vulnerabilities, governance risks, and liquidity constraints.

- Users may face delays or disputes in claim payouts, especially if the incident falls into a gray area not explicitly covered by the policy.

- Policies often exclude losses due to user error, such as sending funds to the wrong address, losing private keys, or falling for phishing attacks.

Examples of Use Cases:

- A DeFi investor providing liquidity on Aave could buy insurance on Nexus Mutual to protect against smart contract exploits.

- A trader holding stablecoins on Coinbase might rely on the exchange's custodial insurance for protection against platform hacks.

- A project issuing tokens on Ethereum could use Unslashed coverage to protect investors' funds from potential protocol bugs or security failures.

While crypto insurance cannot eliminate risk, it provides a safety net that is particularly valuable in the high-risk and rapidly evolving cryptocurrency market. Users should carefully review coverage details, limits, and exclusions, and consider insurance as one layer of risk management alongside secure wallet practices, due diligence, and diversification.

Takeaway: In traditional finance, the government provides the safety net; in crypto, security is largely your responsibility. Insurance can help cover certain risks, but real protection comes from using multiple safeguards—such as cold storage, platform diversification, and careful decision-making.

Chapter 4

How to Get Started?

Choosing a Cryptocurrency Exchange or Broker

Do your research and look for exchanges that prioritize user-friendly applications, strong security practices, transparent fees, and a wide range of supported cryptocurrencies. Keep in mind that not every exchange or broker supports the same digital assets.

Some cryptocurrency exchanges available to U.S. users include *Coinbase, Kraken, eToro*, and *Binance.US*. Availability, features, and supported assets may vary depending on location and regulatory requirements.

What Are Transaction Fees?

Crypto trading platforms generate revenue through various fees that help cover operational costs, liquidity, and network usage.

Standard fees include:

- **Trading & Spread Fees:** Fees charged when executing trades, including commissions and the difference between buy (bid) and sell (ask) prices.

- **Network (Gas) Fees:** Fees paid to blockchain networks to process transactions. These are especially relevant for NFTs (minting or purchasing) and transactions involving smart contracts or utility tokens.

- **Deposit and Withdrawal Fees:** Fees charged for moving assets on or off the platform, often including underlying network costs.

- **Other Fees:** May include inactivity fees or currency conversion fees when exchanging between fiat and cryptocurrencies.

Transaction fees vary widely depending on the cryptocurrency used, network congestion, and platform policies. For many networks, fees can range from $1 to $10, but they may increase significantly during periods of high demand. Ethereum transactions involve gas fees that fluctuate based on network congestion and transaction complexity.

Simple transfers may cost between $0.50 and $30, while more complex smart contract interactions—such as DeFi transactions—can spike to much higher levels during peak usage.

Binance Coin (BNB) transactions typically have lower fees—often between $0.10 and $0.50—particularly when using the *Binance Smart Chain (BSC)*, a blockchain designed for faster and lower-cost transactions.

Other networks known for low fees include *Ripple (XRP)*, *Litecoin* (LTC), and *Solana* (SOL), with transaction costs often ranging from fractions of a cent to a few cents.

DeFi and Smart Contract Fees

Users may incur higher gas fees when interacting with Decentralized Finance (DeFi) platforms or executing smart contracts, especially on networks like Ethereum. Complex activities such as yield farming or minting NFTs require more computational resources, which can result in fees ranging from $5 to $100 or more, depending on network conditions.

Tip: Always check the current network fees before confirming a transaction, especially if you use Ethereum or Bitcoin, as fees fluctuate rapidly.

Choose a User-Friendly Interface and Mobile App

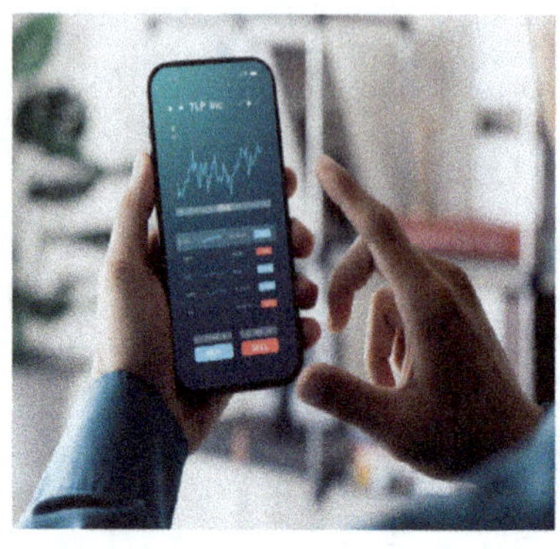

Selecting the right cryptocurrency exchange is crucial for a safe, efficient, and beginner-friendly experience. Look for platforms that offer intuitive dashboards, mobile app availability, and responsive customer support—such as 24/7 chat or email assistance.

Understand how quickly deposits and withdrawals are processed, and review available funding methods, including bank transfers, credit cards, or PayPal. Confirm that the exchange supports the cryptocurrencies you plan to trade and offers sufficient liquidity. Higher trading volumes typically indicate better price execution and easier buying and selling.

Some exchanges also offer peer-to-peer (P2P) trading, which allows users to trade directly with one another—an optional feature that may appeal to certain users.

Research platform reputation by checking reviews on sites like *Trustpilot* or community forums such as *Reddit*. Investigate whether the platform has experienced past security incidents and how they were handled. Select well-established exchanges with strong security records and positive user feedback.

Tip: Don't forget to check user reviews when evaluating a crypto exchange. Platforms like Trustpilot and community discussions on Reddit can provide insight into real user experiences, including customer support, fees, and withdrawal issues.

Create an Account

The next step is to create an account on the crypto exchange you selected. You will usually sign up using your email address and create a strong password. Choose a long password or passphrase that is easy for you to remember but difficult for others to guess. Many exchanges also offer two-factor authentication (2FA), which adds extra protection and is strongly recommended.

Most exchanges require Know Your Customer (KYC) verification before you can trade or withdraw funds. This means you may need to upload a government-issued ID, such as a driver's license or passport, and sometimes confirm your identity with a photo. This process helps prevent fraud and allows exchanges to comply with regulations.

Once your account is approved, you can add funds using a payment method supported by the exchange. Common options include bank transfers (often used for larger amounts with lower fees), credit or debit cards (faster but usually more expensive), and services like *PayPal* or other supported digital wallets.

Security Tip: Always double-check website URLs and emails before entering your login information. Only download exchange apps from official app stores, never share your password or recovery phrase with anyone, and be cautious of messages that pressure you to act quickly—these are common signs of scams.

Setting up a Wallet and Securing Private Keys

First, decide whether you want a **hot wallet** or a **cold wallet** (also called a **hardware wallet**). Hot wallets are connected to the internet and are convenient for everyday use, while cold wallets are designed for long-term storage and offer stronger security because they remain offline.

For beginners, hardware wallets are often recommended for holding larger amounts of cryptocurrency. If you choose a hardware wallet, purchase it **only from the official manufacturer's website** (such as *Ledger* or *Trezor*) to reduce the risk of tampering. After setup, the device can be connected to your computer or mobile device when you need to manage your assets.

> Important clarification: Wallet providers do **not** send you private keys. Instead, your wallet generates them locally during setup. You are solely responsible for safeguarding them.

Some users choose to keep physical backups of their recovery phrase (for example, written on paper or stored in a secure location). This can be helpful, but it must be done carefully to avoid loss, theft, or damage.

Installing a Wallet

Download and install your chosen wallet from official sources only. For mobile wallets, use the official Apple App Store or Google Play Store. For desktop or browser wallets, download directly from the wallet's official website.

Commonly Used Wallets

Mobile wallets include Trust Wallet, MetaMask, and Coinbase Wallet, as well as desktop or browser wallets such as Exodus, Electrum, and MetaMask.

Always double-check the website URL to avoid fake or phishing sites.

When setting up a wallet, you will typically follow these steps:

1. Open the wallet app or device and select "Create a New Wallet."

2. Create a strong password (this applies mainly to hot wallets).

3. Write down your 12–24-word recovery phrase (also called a mnemonic phrase or seed phrase).

A mnemonic phrase is a memory aid—a series of words that represents your wallet's private key. This phrase allows you to recover your wallet and funds if your device is lost, damaged, or replaced.

Never share your recovery phrase or private keys.
Anyone who has access to them has full control over your funds, and transactions on the blockchain cannot be reversed.

How to Secure Your Wallet

To secure your wallet, enable Two-Factor Authentication (2FA) whenever it is available. 2FA requires two forms of verification—such as a password and a one-time code sent to your phone or generated by an authenticator app—before you can log in. This extra layer of protection significantly reduces the risk of unauthorized access.

You should also store your recovery (seed) phrase offline, preferably written on paper and kept in a secure location. Do not store your recovery phrase online, including in email, cloud storage, screenshots, or notes apps, as these can be accessed by hackers. Avoid saving the phrase on a computer or mobile device, since malware or unauthorized access could compromise your funds.

Remember These Wallet Security Do's and Don'ts:

Do:

- Write down your recovery (seed) phrase and store it in a secure, offline location.

- Use a hardware wallet for long-term storage or larger amounts of cryptocurrency.

- Download wallet apps only from official sources, such as the official website or trusted app stores.

- Enable two-factor authentication (2FA) when available, especially for hot wallets and exchanges.

- Keep your wallet software and device updated to protect against known vulnerabilities.

- Double-check addresses before sending crypto—transactions are irreversible.

Don't:

- Do not share your recovery phrase or private keys with anyone—ever.

- Do not store your recovery phrase digitally (screenshots, cloud storage, email, or notes apps).

- Do not click links or download files from unsolicited emails, messages, or social media posts.

- Do not buy hardware wallets from third-party sellers or secondhand marketplaces.

- Do not assume customer support can recover your wallet—they cannot access your keys.

- Do not rush transactions; mistakes cannot be undone on the blockchain.

Adding Cryptocurrency to Your Wallet

The first step in adding cryptocurrency to your wallet is locating your wallet address (public key). This address is used to receive funds, like an account number.

Once you have your wallet address, you can purchase cryptocurrency on the exchange you selected and transfer the funds from the exchange to your wallet for greater security and control.

Before transferring a large amount, it is strongly recommended that you test your wallet with a small transaction. Send a small amount of cryptocurrency to confirm that the address is correct and that the transfer process works as expected. This simple step can help prevent costly mistakes, as blockchain transactions are irreversible.

List of Common Crypto Wallets by Category

Wallet	Type	Best For
MetaMask	Hot (Mobile/ Browser)	Ethereum and Web3 dApps
Trust Wallet	Hot (Mobile)	Multi-crypto support and Binance Smart Chain (BSC)
Exodus	Hot (Mobile and Desktop)	User-friendly experience
Ledger Nano X	Cold (Hardware)	Long term secure storage
Trezor Model T	Cold (Hardware)	Advance security features and offline key storage

As of March 2025

Best Practices for Beginners

The crypto market can offer high returns, but it is highly volatile and carries significant risk. Following best practices can help beginners avoid costly mistakes.

Tips for Safe Trading

1. Stay Informed: Do your research! Follow crypto news, market trends, and insights. Reliable sources include Coingecko.com, CoinDesk.com, CoinMarketCap.com, and Decrypt.co. These sites provide industry news, market data, NFT updates, and beginner guides.

2. Start Small: Begin with small amounts to minimize potential losses while learning the market. Cryptocurrencies differ from traditional stocks and include unique features such as smart contracts, staking, gas fees, and blockchain mechanics. Starting small allows beginners to learn the market dynamics without risking too much.

3. Beware of Scams: Educate yourself about unregulated exchanges and suspicious schemes.

4. If unsure, contact support before completing a transaction. Never share your account details or private keys, even if prompted via email or social media—it is likely a scam.

5. **Diversify Your Portfolio:** Don't invest all your funds in a single cryptocurrency. Diversifying helps reduce risk and protect against market volatility. Consider spreading your investments across multiple types of crypto assets, for example:

   a) Mix **Bitcoin** with **stablecoins**

   b) Include **DeFi assets** like *Uniswap* (UNI) and *Aave* (AAVE)

   c) Add **gaming and metaverse tokens** like *The Sandbox (SAND)* and *Gala (GALA)*

   d) Consider **scalability/network** solutions like *Polygon (MATIC)* and *Cosmos (ATOM)*

   e) Include **privacy coins** like *Monero (XMR)* and *Zcash (ZEC)*

Diversify across blockchains as well, so if one blockchain experiences issues, your other holdings remain unaffected. Popular blockchains for diversification include *Ethereum, Solana, Binance Smart Chain, Cosmos, and Coinbase.*

Crypto Categories for Diversification

Crypto Category	Examples	Purpose in Portfolio
Large-Cap (Stabled) Cryptos	Cryptos, Bitcoin (BTC), Ethereum (ETH)	Stability, long-term growth
Mid-Cap & Emerging	Cryptos, Solana (SOL), Avalanche (AVAX), Chainlink (LINK)	High-growth potential with moderate risk
Stablecoins	USDT, USDC, DAI	Hedge against volatility, liquidity reserve
DeFi (Decentralized Finance),	Uniswap (UNI), Aave (AAVE), Curve (CRV)	Exposure to lending, staking, and swaps
Gaming & Metaverse	Axie Infinity (AXS), The Sandbox (SAND), Gala (GALA)	Investment in blockchain gaming and virtual reality worlds
Layer 1 & Layer 2 Solutions	Polygon (MATIC), Arbitrum (ARB), Cosmos (ATOM)	Scalability and network efficiency
Privacy Coins	Monero (XMR), Zcash (ZEC)	Focus on anonymous transactions

Long-Term Investment vs. Short-Term Trading

Given the unpredictability of the crypto market, beginners should start by focusing on long-term investments rather than short-term trading. Prices can experience extreme fluctuations over short periods, leading to significant losses when trying to time the market. Timing the market means predicting when crypto prices will rise or fall with the intent to buy low and sell high.

For long-term crypto investments (3–10 years), focus on assets with strong fundamentals, real-world utility, and broad adoption. *Stablecoins*, *privacy coins*, and *tokenized assets* are good options for long-term investors. Short-term trading, by contrast, requires the ability to react quickly to market changes, and beginners often lack the experience to manage constant price swings effectively.

Long-term investors can withstand market fluctuations by prioritizing overall portfolio growth potential. For example, if you purchase 3.5 million *Shiba Inu (SHIB)* coins at a fraction of a penny (USD 0.000015 per SHIB), you spend about $200 on the transaction. If the coin's value increases over time, you could make a significant profit. If SHIB rises to $0.50, the value of your coins would exceed $1 million, which could take a few years. However, you also risk losing the initial $200 if the coin is delisted (removed from an exchange).

Short-term crypto investing involves trading and holding assets for days, weeks, or months to capitalize on price movements. Short-term investors typically focus on large-cap cryptocurrencies, which are generally less volatile. However, gains often come from *altcoin* hype cycles, new token launches, or major partnerships.

Meme coins can "pump" quickly but also crash just as fast, making them attractive yet risky for short-term traders. Traders also invest in *stablecoins* and engage in yield farming, which is generally lower risk. Cryptocurrencies like *USDT*, *USDC*, and *DAI* can provide relatively stable short-term gains through staking, lending, or liquidity pools. Some DeFi platforms like *Aave*, *Compound*, or *Binance* offer short-term returns ranging from 5–10% APY (Annual Percentage Yield).

Tip: Focus on long-term holdings with strong fundamentals, test new coins or platforms with small amounts first, diversify and Avoid FOMO—research before chasing hype.

Chapter 5

Buying, Selling, and Trading

After opening an account with a cryptocurrency broker (also called a "crypto exchange"), you can download the exchange's mobile application. The exchange website typically provides step-by-step instructions for downloading the app and setting up your account.

Next, set up your account, which is usually free of charge. You will need to fund it by connecting your bank account or adding credit/debit card details. Once your account is funded, you can start buying Bitcoin or altcoins.

You don't have to buy a whole coin—you can purchase a fraction. For example, spending $200 on Bitcoin allows you to own a proportional share of BTC if you can't afford a full unit.

Buying Cryptocurrency

Once your account is funded, you can place an order in one of two ways. A **market order** executes immediately at the best available price, while a **limit order** executes only when the asset reaches a specific price you set.

After purchasing crypto, transfer your funds to a private wallet for enhanced security and follow these guidelines to help ensure a secure investment and mitigate risk. Research the project by investigating the coin's use case, team, roadmap, and community support to avoid scams or unreliable ventures. Check regulations and taxes, as some cryptocurrencies may have legal restrictions or tax implications in your country and ensure compliance before purchasing. Prioritize security by using reputable exchanges with two-factor authentication and storing assets in hardware or non-custodial wallets to protect against cyberattacks. Understand volatility, as the crypto market can fluctuate significantly, and maintain a clear investment strategy. Equally important is recognizing that many losses occur not from market forces but from fraudulent activity.

Finally, **beware of scams** such as social engineering attacks, rug pulls, and phishing attempts; staying informed and cautious reduces risk.

Selling Cryptocurrency: Initiating the Sell Order

To sell your cryptocurrency, you must first transfer it to your exchange wallet—if it is stored in an external wallet. Most centralized exchanges (CEX), such as *Binance, Coinbase,* and *Kraken,* require cryptocurrencies to be in their platform wallets to process a sale.

When using a **decentralized exchange (DEX)**, you can sell directly from your private wallet. Some **P2P** platforms allow wallet-to-wallet transactions. You may not need an exchange wallet if using **crypto ATMs** or **over-the-counter (OTC)** trades.

Before placing a sell order, consider several factors:

- Market research: Track price trends, news, and events that can impact cryptocurrency values.

- Order type: Choose between a market order or a limit order.

- Transaction fees: Fees differ by exchange and can impact final earnings. Review fees ahead of time.

- Liquidity: Low-volume cryptocurrencies may take longer to sell.

- Taxes: Consult a tax professional, as selling cryptocurrencies may trigger capital gains taxes in many jurisdictions.

How to Sell: A Step-by-Step Walkthrough

The process of selling crypto is straightforward and can be easily navigated by following these steps:

1. Log in to your account and navigate to the trading or sell section.

2. Select the cryptocurrency you want to sell.

3. Choose the order type: market or limit.

4. Enter the amount to sell.

5. Review transaction details carefully, including fees and expected returns.

6. Confirm and execute the sale.

7. Withdraw fiat currency (e.g., USD or EUR) to your bank account if desired.

Following these steps and staying informed about market trends and security practices can help ensure a smooth transaction experience.

Withdrawing Funds

Users can transfer or withdraw fiat currency (e.g., USD, EUR) from a crypto exchange to their **bank account** or **e-wallet**. Always follow the instructions provided by your exchange carefully. Keep in mind that withdrawal fees, limits, and processing times vary by exchange and can affect how quickly you receive your funds.

Crypto ATMs

Crypto ATMs—sometimes called Bitcoin ATMs—allow users to convert cryptocurrency into cash. The withdrawal process typically involves:

1. Selecting the **"Sell"** or **"Withdraw"** option on the ATM.

2. Choosing the cryptocurrency and specifying the amount.

3. Sending the requested crypto to the wallet address or scanning the QR code displayed on the ATM.

4. Waiting for the blockchain to confirm the transaction. Once confirmed, the ATM dispenses the corresponding cash amount, minus any transaction fees.

Crypto ATMs provide a convenient way to buy or sell cryptocurrency, but not all machines support cash withdrawals. Fees can be higher than those on online exchanges, particularly for smaller transactions. Depending on the operator and local regulations, identity verification may be required for larger withdrawals.

Additionally, blockchain confirmation times can vary, so users may need to wait several minutes—or longer during periods of network congestion—before receiving their cash.

Best Practices for Withdrawing Funds:

- Double-check details: Verify the wallet address, cryptocurrency type, and withdrawal amount before confirming the transaction. Mistakes can result in permanent loss of funds.

- Keep records: Save receipts or transaction confirmations for your personal records and tax purposes.

- Understand tax implications: Converting cryptocurrency into cash or fiat currency may trigger taxable events in your jurisdiction. Consult a tax professional to ensure compliance.

- Compare options: Check withdrawal fees and processing times for different methods (bank transfer, e-wallet, ATM) to minimize costs.

By following these steps and precautions, users can safely convert crypto into cash while avoiding common errors, unexpected fees, or delays.

Trading Cryptocurrency

Before trading cryptocurrencies, it's important to understand the basics and key concepts such as market orders, limit orders, and stop-loss orders. Choosing a trading platform optimized for your needs, such as *Coinbase, Kraken, or Binance*—is your first step. Unlike traditional financial markets with set hours, crypto trading is available 24/7. While this creates opportunities to take advantage of market movements at any time, the continuous nature of the market also increases risk due to volatility.

The cryptocurrency market is challenging to predict, as it is influenced by global economic conditions, regulatory news, and technological developments. Security should always be a top priority. Traders must protect their assets using secure wallets and reputable exchanges.

Staying informed about news and developments helps make better trading decisions. Smaller cryptocurrencies are often more volatile due to lower market capitalization, making it important to consider liquidity and risk before trading.

Crypto traders employ different strategies depending on their goals and experience:

- Day trading: Buying and selling assets within the same day to gain small profits from temporary price swings.

- Swing trading: Capitalizing on market fluctuations over several days or weeks by buying low and selling high.

- Scalping: Executing multiple small trades within minutes or hours to profit from minor price movements.

Technical indicators are commonly used to guide trading decisions. These include:

- Moving averages: Track the average price of a cryptocurrency over a specific period.

- Relative Strength Index (RSI): Measures the speed and magnitude of price changes to identify overbought or oversold conditions.

- Fibonacci charts: Analyze potential support and resistance levels to anticipate price movements.

The diagram below illustrates a trade in which Emma sends Bitcoin (BTC) to Lucas and receives Ethereum (ETH) in return.

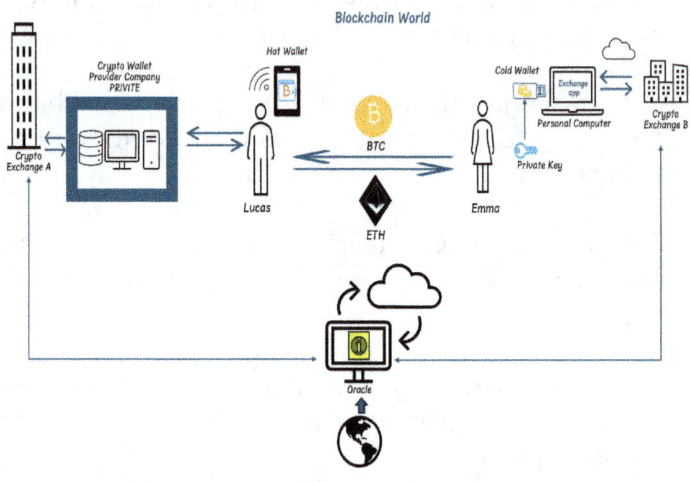
Blockchain World
Crypto Wallet Provider Company PRIVITE
Hot Wallet
Cold Wallet
Exchange app
Personal Computer
Crypto Exchange B
Crypto Exchange A
BTC
Private Key
Lucas
Emma
ETH
Oracle

How to Perform Market Analysis?

Crypto market analysis helps traders and investors make informed decisions rather than guessing price movements.

There are three main types of analysis:

1. Technical Analysis (TA)

Technical analysis uses charts and patterns to predict price movements. This method examines price trends, trading volume, moving averages, and whether a crypto asset is oversold or overbought. It helps identify key price points and potential trend reversals. Common tools include platforms such as TradingView for advanced charting and indicators, CryptoQuant and Glassnode for on-chain data analysis, IntoTheBlock for AI-driven market analytics, and Coinalyze for derivatives data, open interest, and liquidation metrics.

2. Fundamental Analysis (FA)

Fundamental analysis evaluates a cryptocurrency's real-world applications, use cases, and long-term potential.

It considers the project's technology, purpose, token supply, staking rewards, and burning mechanisms. Adoption trends, ecosystem growth, and community engagement on platforms such as Reddit or Discord can indicate future demand. Frequently used resources include CoinMarketCap and CoinGecko for market data and tokenomics, Messari for in-depth research and reports, Santiment for social sentiment and on-chain data, and Token Unlocks for tracking vesting schedules and supply releases.

3. Sentiment Analysis

Sentiment analysis examines trader and investor emotions to gauge market confidence. Indicators may include the Fear & Greed Index, social media trends, Google search trends, and funding rates, where positive rates typically signal bullish sentiment and negative rates indicate bearish sentiment. Tools commonly used for sentiment analysis include Alternative.me for the Fear & Greed Index, LunarCrush for tracking social media and influencer activity, and Google Trends for monitoring search interest in cryptocurrency topics.

A strong crypto market analysis strategy combines technical, fundamental, and sentiment analysis. Using multiple approaches together can provide a more comprehensive understanding of market dynamics and improve trading or investment decisions.

Tip: Combine technical, fundamental, and sentiment analysis to gain a full view of the crypto market, make informed decisions, and reduce risk.

Cryptocurrency Trading Best Practices

When getting started with crypto, it helps to focus on a few key habits. By applying three simple principles—diversifying your portfolio, managing your risk, and staying informed—you'll be in a much better position to protect your money and make smarter trading decisions.

1. Diversify Your Portfolio

Don't put all your money into a single cryptocurrency. A balanced portfolio can reduce risk and improve long-term potential. For example:

- 60% – Bitcoin & Ethereum (strong, long-term assets).

- 25% – Altcoins (higher growth potential, but riskier).

- 10% – DeFi, NFTs, and Web3 projects (emerging opportunities).

- 5% – Stablecoins (USDT, USDC) for liquidity and risk management.

2. Manage Risk and Protect Your Capital

Invest only what you can afford to lose, as crypto is highly volatile. Use stop-loss orders to automatically sell assets if they drop to a set price, and take profits regularly by selling portions when prices rise.

Watch for scams and rug pulls—situations where project creators suddenly abandon a project and disappear with investor funds. Be cautious of projects with no security audits or anonymous teams. Store assets securely in hardware wallets such as Ledger or Trezor, and practice trading with small amounts before committing larger funds.

Crypto simulation platforms, such as **Investopedia Simulator**, **Crypto Parrot**, and **Bitsgap Demo Mode**, allow beginners to trade virtual assets with real or simulated market data. This helps users gain experience without risking real money.

3. Stay Informed and Adapt

Track market trends using reputable tools such as CoinGecko and *CoinMarketCap*. Follow crypto news from *CoinDesk* and The Block, and monitor on-chain analytics with *Glassnode* or *CryptoQuant*. Staying informed helps you spot trends and make better trading decisions.

Understand Cryptocurrency Risk Factors

Before investing, evaluate the key risks associated with crypto assets:

- **Adoption Risk** – Risk that a project fails to gain users or market traction.

- **Technology Risk** – Bugs, network failures, or protocol vulnerabilities.

- **Market Risk** – Price volatility and liquidity fluctuations.

- **Security Risk** – Hacks, phishing attacks, or compromised wallets.

- **Regulatory Risk** – Changes in laws, taxation, or government restrictions.

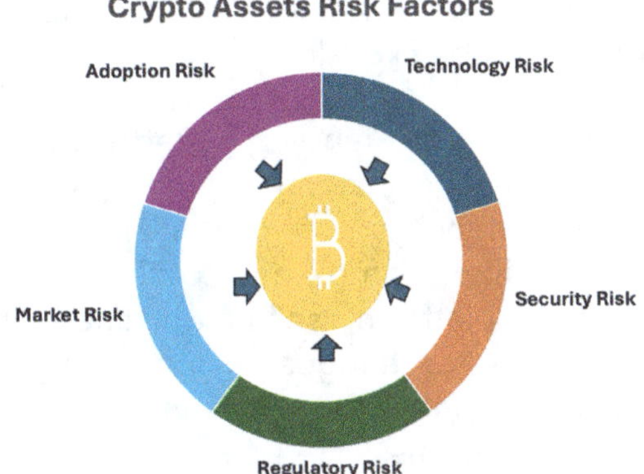

How to Generate Passive Income in the Crypto Market?

Investors can generate passive income in the crypto market by leveraging blockchain-based opportunities and financial instruments that earn rewards over time. There are several ways to earn passive income in cryptocurrency, each with its own mechanisms, platforms, potential returns, and associated risks.

Staking is a common method where investors temporarily lock their cryptocurrency in a blockchain network to support transaction validation and earn rewards. **Yield farming** involves providing liquidity to Decentralized Finance (DeFi) protocols in exchange for interest or governance tokens.

Lending platforms allow crypto holders to lend their assets to borrowers in return for interest payments. Some projects pay dividends or share revenue, enabling token holders to receive regular payments. Additionally, investors can run a **masternode**, a specialized server that participates in network operations and governance, generating income while supporting the blockchain.

Many exchanges and lending platforms also offer interest-bearing savings accounts, where users can earn returns by simply depositing crypto. While these methods can generate passive income, they come with risks such as market volatility, platform security vulnerabilities, and potential regulatory changes. Conducting thorough research and diversifying income streams can help mitigate risks and maximize returns.

Beyond just holding a digital asset, there are several ways to participate in the ecosystem and earn rewards:

1. Staking

- How it works: Staking involves holding and locking a specific amount of cryptocurrency in a blockchain network that uses a Proof-of-Stake (PoS) consensus mechanism. In return for helping secure the network and validate transactions, stakers earn rewards, typically in additional tokens.

- Platforms: Many PoS-based blockchains offer staking opportunities. Centralized exchanges like Binance and Coinbase also provide staking services for various cryptocurrencies.

- Potential returns: Staking rewards vary by network and amount staked. For example, staking Ether (ETH) can yield an annual return of over 3.2% (MarketWatch, January 2025).

- Risks: Staking requires locking assets for a certain period, limiting liquidity. Risks include network vulnerabilities, token price fluctuations, or changes in protocol rules.

2. Yield Farming

- How it works: Also called liquidity mining, yield farming involves providing crypto assets to liquidity pools on DeFi protocols. In exchange, investors earn interest or additional tokens.

- Platforms: Popular platforms include *Uniswap*, *Compound*, and *Aave*.

- Potential returns: Returns can be substantial but vary widely depending on the platform and specific pool.

- Risks: Yield farming carries high risk, including coding errors, hacks, and market volatility. The DeFi space is relatively new and can be unstable.

3. Crypto Lending

- How it works: Lending platforms allow users to lend digital assets to borrowers in exchange for interest payments.

- Platforms: Centralized platforms like BlockFi and Nexo, as well as decentralized protocols like Aave, facilitate crypto lending.

- Potential returns: Interest rates vary by platform and crypto, typically ranging from 3% to over 10% annually.

- Risks: Risks include borrower default, platform insolvency, and security breaches.

4. Play-to-Earn Games

- How it works: Players earn cryptocurrency or NFTs by participating in a game's ecosystem.

- Platforms: *Axie Infinity* popularized this model, where players collect, breed, and battle digital creatures called Axies.

- Potential returns: Earnings depend on in-game achievements and market demand for assets.

- Risks: The play-to-earn model is speculative and volatile, relying heavily on a constant influx of new players.

5. Real Estate Tokenization

- How it works: Real estate tokenization divides physical property into digital tokens, allowing investors to own fractional shares and earn rental income or benefit from property appreciation.

- Platforms: Platforms like *Lofty* and *HouseBit* provide tokenized real estate investments.

- Potential returns: Returns are like traditional real estate but depend on property performance and market conditions.

- Risks: Risks include limited liquidity, property management issues, and regulatory uncertainties.

Each of these methods offers unique opportunities for earning passive income in the crypto market. However, all come with risks. Consider your risk tolerance, research carefully, and diversify your strategies before participating.

Chapter 6

Cryptocurrency Security and Risks

Decentralization is a key benefit of the cryptocurrency market because it reduces reliance on a single central authority and increases transparency. It also creates opportunities for innovation and potential high returns. However, decentralization introduces unique security risks that stem from both technical vulnerabilities and human behavior. Individuals and businesses must understand these risks and take proactive steps to manage them. Because cryptocurrencies operate in a digital and decentralized environment, security awareness is critical for investors and traders. Understanding common threats can help prevent financial losses caused by scams, hacks, and system failures.

Below are some of the most significant security risks associated with cryptocurrency.

Hacking, Scams, and Cyberattacks

Cryptocurrency exchanges and platforms are frequent targets for hackers because they often hold large amounts of digital assets. One of the most notable incidents occurred in 2014 with the collapse of Mt. Gox, which at the time handled over 70% of all Bitcoin trades. The exchange lost approximately 850,000 Bitcoin (BTC), highlighting the risks of weak internal controls and security practices.

Decentralized applications (dApps) rely on smart contracts, which can also be exploited if they are poorly written or insufficiently audited. A well-known example is *The DAO* hack in June 2016. *The DAO*, a decentralized investment fund built on the Ethereum blockchain, was exploited through a code vulnerability.

The attacker stole approximately 3.6 million Ether (ETH)—about one-third of the funds raised—into a separate account.

At the time, the loss was valued at roughly $50–$70 million, and the incident ultimately led to Ethereum's historic hard fork. A hard fork is when a blockchain splits into two separate versions, creating a permanent change in its rules. This can happen to fix a major issue, like recovering stolen funds, or to upgrade the network. In this case, Ethereum's hard fork was designed to reverse the stolen funds from The DAO hack, while the original blockchain continued as Ethereum Classic.

Beyond large-scale hacks, scams such as fake investment schemes, impersonation attacks, and fraudulent token offerings continue to target unsuspecting users, especially beginners.

Network Attacks

Network attacks attempt to disrupt or manipulate blockchain operations rather than targeting individual users directly.

A 51% attack occurs when a single entity or group gains control of more than half of a blockchain's computing power or staking influence. This allows attackers to reverse transactions, double-spend coins, or prevent new transactions from being confirmed. Smaller or less secure blockchains are particularly vulnerable to this type of attack.

A Sybil attack involves an attacker creating multiple fake identities to gain disproportionate influence over a network. This can disrupt consensus mechanisms or degrade network reliability.

A Distributed Denial-of-Service (DDoS) attack floods a cryptocurrency exchange or blockchain service with excessive traffic, causing outages or delays that prevent users from accessing their funds or completing transactions.

Another common threat is phishing attacks, where attackers impersonate legitimate platforms through fake websites, emails, or messages to trick users into revealing private keys, recovery phrases, or login credentials. Once compromised, wallets can be drained almost instantly.

Because of blockchain's decentralized and irreversible nature, stolen cryptocurrency is rarely recoverable after an attack. As a result, strong security practices—such as using reputable platforms, enabling multi-factor authentication (MFA), safeguarding private keys, and remaining vigilant against scams—are essential to reducing risk and protecting digital assets.

Phishing Attacks

Phishing attacks have caused significant losses in the crypto market. According to the ABA Banking Journal, the FBI (Federal Bureau of Investigation) reported that in 2023, crypto-related fraud resulted in losses of **$5.6 billion**, a 45% increase from the previous year.

Crypto users are frequent targets because attackers often mimic legitimate services, such as wallet providers, exchanges, or even well-known crypto personalities. These scams can happen through **email, social media, fake websites, or over the phone.** Hackers may create clone websites that look identical to real cryptocurrency platforms. Unsuspecting users who enter their credentials or send funds to these fraudulent platforms can lose their assets immediately.

Malicious mobile apps also pose a risk. Some apps appear legitimate but ask for private keys, passwords, or other sensitive information, which is then stolen. Even experienced users can fall victim if they aren't careful, making awareness and double-checking all platforms critical for security.

Tip: Phishing scams rely on urgency and fake trust—never click links from emails or texts, claiming there's a "problem" with your wallet or exchange. Always go directly to the official website yourself and remember: no legitimate crypto platform will ever ask for your private keys or recovery phrase.

Loss of Private Keys

In crypto, your private key is like the key to your treasure chest. If it's lost or stolen, your cryptocurrency is gone forever. Unlike traditional banks, there's no safety net, no customer service to recover it—it's all on you.

Hot wallets (online wallets) are convenient but connected to the internet, making them more vulnerable to hacks. Hackers can drain funds in real time if they access an exchange or wallet.

Hardware wallets are safer, but they can be lost, stolen, or damaged. Without a proper backup, access to your crypto may be permanently lost.

Tip: Always back up your private keys in multiple secure locations, and never share them with anyone.

Rug Pull and Ponzi Schemes

A rug pull happens when developers of a crypto project or DeFi protocol take all the funds from investors and disappear. Many new tokens and DeFi projects are unregulated, making them easy targets for scammers.

The Squid Game Token (SQUID) in 2021is a classic example of a rug pull scam. Its hype caused the price to skyrocket to $2,861 per token—but the developers drained liquidity, and the token crashed to nearly zero. Investors lost over $3.3 million.

Pump-and-dump schemes occur when fraudsters artificially drive up the price of a cryptocurrency (the "pump") and then quickly sell their holdings (the "dump"), leaving other investors with significant losses. These schemes are more common in loosely regulated markets and have been reported in regions such as the Bahamas, Bermuda, Argentina, and Turkey. Always be cautious of hype-driven promotions—if an investment sounds too good to be true, it probably is.

In 2024, the Fronk (Solana Meme Coin) project raised over $500,000 and then disappeared, deleting all social media accounts. Globally, crypto scams led to **$9.9 billion in losses** in 2024. Americans lost about **$3.9 billion**, and Singapore reported at least **$1.1 billion in scams**, including a single victim losing $125 million.

The cryptocurrency market is unpredictable and still largely unregulated, which makes it an attractive target for fraudsters. Scammers exploit investors through tactics such as rug pulls, Ponzi schemes, phishing attacks, and pump-and-dump schemes. Staying informed about these common scams is essential for protecting your investments and avoiding unnecessary financial losses.

Tip: Be cautious of sudden hype, social media pressure, or "can't-miss" deals—real opportunities don't rush you or promise easy money.

Social Engineering Attacks

Social engineering is a type of manipulation where attackers trick people into giving up sensitive information—such as passwords, private keys, or access to accounts—by exploiting trust, fear, urgency, or curiosity rather than breaking into systems using technical methods.

Examples of common social engineering tactics include:

- Fake customer support scams: Scammers create fake MetaMask or exchange support pages, guiding users to reveal their seed phrases.

- Phishing attacks: Hackers imitate legitimate exchanges or wallets via fake websites, emails, or social media messages. Users enter private keys, losing access to their funds.

- Impersonation scams: Fraudsters pose as influencers or company employees, promising giveaways or urgent assistance. Victims send crypto to scammers' wallets, expecting a reward.

- Honeypot smart contracts: Tokens appear profitable but have hidden code that prevents withdrawals.

- **Pretexting attacks**: Scammers build trust over time by pretending to be advisors or friends, then convince victims to send crypto.

Crypto communities on **Discord and Telegram** are common targets. Scammers may pose as admins, tricking users into connecting wallets to malicious contracts.

As we explore more sophisticated scams in the crypto space, one emerging threat stands out for its long-term manipulation tactics: the "**pig butchering**" scam. Pig butchering crypto scams involve long-term relationship-building via dating apps or social media. Scammers eventually lure victims into fake exchanges or investments. The victim deposits money into a fake exchange or trading platform, only to realize later that they cannot withdraw their funds. This scam has caused billions of dollars in losses globally.

These incidents emphasize the urgent need for vigilance, skepticism towards unsolicited offers, and robust security practices.

Tip: Never share your private keys or seed phrases—not even with helpdesk staff. Always verify official websites and accounts before taking any action.

Celebrity and Influencer Scams

Some scams exploit celebrities or influencers to promote fake tokens or investment opportunities, leading to financial losses for their followers. Fraudsters use the names, videos and images of well-known figures that appear legitimate. These scams can occur in various forms, such as fake endorsements, impersonations, and hijacked social media accounts.

A notorious case was the "Ethereum giveaway" scam, where impersonators posing as Vitalik Buterin and other crypto leaders promised to double any Ethereum sent to their wallet, only to disappear with the funds.

Some celebrities have unknowingly promoted fraudulent crypto projects and faced legal action for endorsing fraudulent Initial Coin Offerings (ICOs) that later collapsed. When well-known figures are involved, these scams can appear legitimate, tricking unsuspecting investors into losing their money.

Tip: Always check that endorsements are genuine, and don't send crypto based on a social media post alone.

Vulnerabilities in Consensus Mechanisms

Proof Cryptocurrencies rely on mechanisms like **Proof of Work (PoW)** or **Proof of Stake (PoS)** to secure networks. They both come with their own inherent vulnerabilities.

Proof of Work (PoW) – used by Bitcoin, relies on miners solving complex math problems with powerful computers to validate transactions. Mining pools (groups of miners working together) could gain too much control over the network, potentially allowing them to manipulate transactions or block others. This makes smaller blockchains especially vulnerable. A successful attack could lead to stolen funds, loss of trust, and significant price drops.

PoS (Proof of Stake) – used by Ethereum 2.0, allows validators to lock up (stake) their cryptocurrency to help secure the network. Large stakeholders might gain too much influence, and "nothing at stake" attacks can occur—this is when validators try to approve multiple competing versions of the blockchain at the same time because they don't risk losing their staked coins. This can undermine trust in the network and make it less secure. This can also create confusion about which transactions are valid and potentially cause financial losses for investors.

If validators try to approve multiple competing blockchains without risking their staked coins, it can lead to a "fork," where the blockchain splits into two versions. This can create confusion about which transactions are valid and may result in financial losses for investors.

While there are other consensus methods emerging in the crypto space, most are adaptations of Proof of Work or Proof of Stake. For beginners, understanding these two main types is enough to grasp how blockchains validate transactions and what risks to watch for.

Tip: Understand how the network you invest in is secured, and stay aware of potential vulnerabilities.

Privacy and Anonymity

Many people think crypto is fully anonymous, but most transactions are **pseudonymous**, meaning they are linked to wallet addresses instead of real names. While identities aren't shown, all Bitcoin and Ethereum transactions are still publicly visible on the blockchain.

Law enforcement and other entities like the FBI can use blockchain analysis tools to trace transactions, potentially leading to the identification of individuals behind crypto wallets. In 2013, Ross Ulbricht, creator of Silk Road—a marketplace designed for the dark web that uses Bitcoin as a form of payment, was arrested through Bitcoin transaction tracking and sentenced to life in prison.

Ransomware groups like *REvil* and *DarkSide* have also been caught this way, and several members have been arrested. Ransomware groups like REvil and DarkSide operate by breaking into computer systems, encrypting files so they become unusable, and then demanding payment—usually in cryptocurrency—to unlock them. These groups often target large organizations such as hospitals, energy companies, and government agencies, where downtime can be extremely costly.

For example, DarkSide was responsible for the 2021 Colonial Pipeline attack, which temporarily disrupted fuel supplies across parts of the United States.

Although these criminals rely on cryptocurrency believing it is untraceable, law enforcement agencies use blockchain analysis tools to follow the movement of ransom payments on public blockchains.

In several cases, investigators were able to trace payments back to wallets controlled by criminal organizations, identify individuals involved, and make arrests.

These cases show that crypto leaves a permanent digital trail that authorities can analyze and use to hold criminals accountable.

Human Error and Operational Risks

Mistakes can be costly: sending crypto to the wrong address, entering the wrong key, or skipping verification steps can permanently lose funds.

A legendary example is the case of **James Howells**, who accidentally threw away a hard drive containing over 8,000 BTC—worth over $500 million in 2025.

Don't forget to verify transaction details. A mistake can result in irreversible financial losses. Unlike credit card purchases, cryptocurrency transactions cannot be reversed once processed.

Crypto investors holding large portfolios are advised to use a multisignature wallet. A *multisignature (multisig)* wallet is a crypto wallet that requires approval from more than one private key to complete a transaction.

Instead of one person having full control, multiple trusted parties must agree before funds can be moved, which adds an extra layer of security and helps prevent theft, mistakes, or unauthorized access.

Tip: Always Double-check addresses and keys before sending transactions.

Environmental Risks

Cryptocurrency environmental risks are primarily due to the energy-intensive process of mining for proof-of-work (PoW) blockchains like Bitcoin. Mining requires huge amounts of computational power.

This leads to excessive electricity consumption which contributes to carbon emissions and impacts climate change and the rapid turnover of mining hardware results in electronic waste, since outdated equipment is frequently discarded.

Some blockchain networks, such as Ethereum, have transitioned to proof-of-stake (PoS) consensus mechanisms, which significantly reduce energy consumption compared to proof-of-work systems. However, Ethereum and other PoS networks still rely on data centers, infrastructure, and global network activity that consume energy.

Bitcoin and other PoW-based cryptocurrencies remain far more energy-intensive and continue to raise major sustainability concerns. As a result, energy use and environmental impact remain ongoing issues in the crypto industry, and certain cryptocurrencies may be affected by future regulations aimed at reducing carbon emissions and overall energy consumption.

While there are ongoing efforts to incorporate renewable energy and carbon offset initiatives into crypto mining, the overall environmental footprint of the industry continues to pose a significant challenge.

Tip: Check if a cryptocurrency uses Proof-of-Stake (PoS) if you're concerned about energy use.

Regulatory Risks

As Bitcoin's price soared, governments began to view cryptocurrencies as both a financial instrument and a potential threat. Legal uncertainty has become a significant concern for investors, as the legal status of cryptocurrencies varies widely across different countries and regions. While some nations have imposed outright bans or strict regulations on crypto, others have adopted a more lenient approach.

This can create regulatory risk, where changes in law or regulations can affect the value of specific cryptocurrencies or even lead to confiscation or other legal repercussions like enforcement actions.

Cryptocurrencies are taxed in many jurisdictions, but the rules can be unclear or inconsistent. Failure to comply with local tax laws or to report cryptocurrency holdings properly could result in penalties or legal issues for individuals or businesses.

After Bitcoin's price drop in 2017, governments worldwide tightened regulations. In 2018, the Securities Exchange commission (SEC) declared that many ICOs were unregistered securities, making them illegal. Major lawsuits followed, shutting down fraudulent projects.

In 2019, crypto taxation enforcement increased. The IRS sent warning letters to thousands of crypto traders, demanding unpaid taxes. In 2023 the Internal Revenue Service (IRS) expanded crypto tax reporting, requiring exchanges to report transactions like stockbrokers. The SEC sued major exchanges (Binance & Coinbase) for allegedly selling unregistered securities.

The rise of Decentralized Finance (DeFi) and NFTs makes regulation tricky, but staying informed is key to compliance. One thing is certain: crypto taxation and regulatory oversight will continue to evolve. Those who ignore the rules risk penalties, while those who adapt will thrive in the new regulated space.

Exchanges and blockchains can reduce security risk by auditing smart contracts code practices and their platforms and providing security training to their employees and users to keep them up to date with cryptocurrency security best practices and aware of new vulnerabilities or threats in the cryptocurrency ecosystem.

Unchecked cryptocurrency security risks can have significant financial and operational consequences, but with proper precautions, many of these risks can be mitigated. Crypto risks can be costly, but careful practices and staying alert can protect your funds

Tip: Understand the regulatory and tax rules that apply in your country. Use reputable exchanges, keep clear records of your transactions, and stay informed about regulatory changes, as compliance requirements can shift quickly and directly affect your assets.

Crypto Security Guide for Beginners

If you're new to crypto, security should be your first priority. This quick guide breaks down the most common risks and simple steps you can take to protect your crypto from scams, hacks, and avoidable losses.

1. **Protect Your Private Keys** – Your private key is your wallet's password. Never share it and always keep backups in safe, offline locations.

2. **Use Hardware Wallets for Large Holdings** – Hot wallets (online) are convenient but vulnerable. Hardware wallets reduce hacking risk.

3. **Avoid Rug Pulls & Ponzi Schemes** – If a crypto project promises huge returns fast, be suspicious. Verify official sources before investing.

4. **Beware of Social Engineering** – Scammers may pose as support staff, influencers, or friends. Always verify identities before sending crypto.

5. Don't Fall for Celebrity Scams – Fake endorsements or "giveaways" can steal your funds. Check legitimacy carefully.

6. Understand Consensus Risks – Know if your coin uses Proof of Work or Proof of Stake and the vulnerabilities involved.

7. Privacy ≠ Anonymity – Most blockchains are public. Use privacy coins only if you understand the risks.

8. Double-Check Transactions – Mistakes like sending crypto to the wrong address are permanent. Always confirm details before sending.

9. Consider Environmental Impact – Mining PoW coins consumes a lot of energy. Research the sustainability of your investments.

10. Stay Updated on Regulations – Laws and taxes vary. Keep up with your local rules to avoid penalties.

Tip: Vigilance + education = safer investing. One small precaution today can prevent big losses tomorrow.

Is Investing in Cryptocurrency Safe?

You're probably eager to know the answer. The short answer is it **depends** on how you **invest**. Cryptocurrency can be both safe and risky, depending on your knowledge, strategy, and tolerance for risk.

The crypto market offers opportunities for growth when approached with the right precautions. However, because of its volatility and evolving regulations, it is best suited for investors who are willing to learn and stay informed. Many people have made significant profits over time by maintaining a balanced portfolio, but prices can also change rapidly. Government regulations continue to evolve, and their long-term impact on crypto markets is still uncertain.

Security is another important consideration. Hackers and scammers frequently target exchanges and digital wallets, and unlike traditional financial systems, crypto transactions usually cannot be reversed. There are no standard refunds or chargebacks if funds are lost, which makes personal responsibility critical.

Crypto investing can offer high potential returns, but it is not inherently stable. Beginners should start with small amounts and focus on continuous education.

Only invest money you can afford to lose—funds that will not affect your day-to-day living or financial stability. Smaller and lesser-known cryptocurrencies are especially prone to extreme price swings.

Takeaway: Cryptocurrency investing is not inherently safe or unsafe—it is shaped by how informed, prepared, and cautious you are. Understanding volatility, security risks, and regulatory uncertainty is essential before investing. Starting small, staying educated, and only committing funds you can afford to lose helps reduce exposure to unnecessary risk.

Cryptocurrency prices are influenced by many factors, including supply and demand, news events, regulations, market sentiment, and actions by large institutions. Managing these risks requires staying informed, setting clear strategies, and avoiding emotional decision-making. Reliable sources such as CoinDesk and tools like LunarCrush can help you track news and market sentiment.

Without proper security knowledge, investors risk losing funds to scams, hacks, or simple mistakes. Understanding basic security practices is essential for safer investing and long-term protection in the crypto space.

Tips for Managing Market Risk

1. Use stop-loss orders to limit losses and automatically sell or buy cryptocurrency when it reaches a set price.
2. Invest only what you can truly afford to lose! It's essential to protect your finances while pursuing opportunities.
3. Stick to a clear strategy and adjust it as market conditions change.
4. Monitor price changes and adjust your positions as needed.

Tip: Understand the project before investing and don't put all your money in one coin!

Chapter 7

Mining and Energy Costs Associated with Crypto

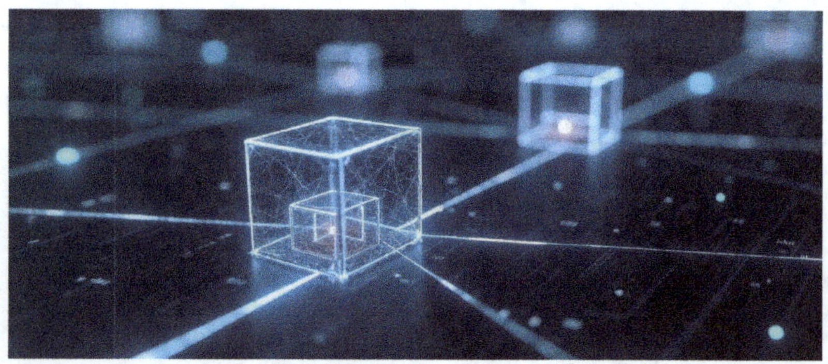

Basics of Cryptocurrency Mining and PoW

The Blockchain networks are designed to prioritize security and decentralization, making it difficult for any single entity to control the transaction records. Transactions are verified and added to the blockchain, and new coins are created through a process known as Proof of Work (PoW).

Mining requires powerful computers that consume large amounts of electricity. These energy costs can influence cryptocurrency prices, as miners may need to sell coins at higher prices to remain profitable. One key indicator of a network's strength is its **hash rate**, which measures how much computing power is being used to process transactions. A higher hash rate generally signals a more secure network and can increase investor confidence.

A hash can be thought of as a digital "guess." The hash rate represents how many of these guesses are made every second. In large networks like Bitcoin, miners compete by making trillions of guesses per second to solve a cryptographic puzzle.

To put this into perspective, imagine a massive lottery that happens every 10 minutes. Thousands of participants (miners) compete to guess a special winning number. Each participant uses specialized machines capable of making millions or trillions of guesses per second.

The first miner to guess the correct number wins the lottery. In cryptocurrency terms, this miner successfully **mines a block** and receives a reward in digital coins. Once a block is mined, the process restarts, and miners begin competing again for the next block. In this way, Proof of Work functions like a continuous guessing game.

This process helps secure the blockchain because solving these puzzles requires real time and energy, making it extremely difficult to fake or manipulate transactions.

It also controls how new coins enter circulation, ensuring they are earned through computation rather than created out of thin air. New coins are issued as rewards for successfully solving these puzzles.

The difficulty of these puzzles adjusts automatically based on the number of miners participating. This ensures that blocks are added at a steady and predictable pace. On the Bitcoin network, for example, a new block is added approximately every 10 minutes.

Miners serve as the backbone of the Bitcoin network. They validate transactions, prevent double-spending, control the release of new coins, and help maintain network stability by confirming transactions at a consistent rate.

Tip: Mining uses massive energy and can affect crypto prices. Understanding these costs helps you see why some cryptocurrencies are more expensive and why energy-efficient networks matter.

Environmental Concerns and Energy Efficiency

Cryptocurrency mining, especially with the **Proof of Work (PoW)** mechanism, has raised significant environmental concerns in recent years. The main issues are the energy consumption and carbon emissions associated with mining operations, particularly for Bitcoin, and the broader sustainability of these activities.

Bitcoin's PoW system is famously energy-intensive. In 2025, Bitcoin is projected to consume around 175.87 terawatt-hours (TWh) of electricity per year, roughly equivalent to the annual power usage of a country like Poland. To put this in perspective, an average Bitcoin transaction uses approximately 1,252 kWh of electricity—enough to power a typical U.S. household for over a month.

A 2021 study by **Selectra** highlighted the efficiency gap between cryptocurrencies and traditional payment systems. For example, the same energy required for 1,000 kWh could process more than 770,000 Visa credit card transactions, showing the massive difference in energy efficiency.

Efforts are underway to reduce the environmental footprint of cryptocurrency mining. These include proposals for climate taxes, relocation of mining operations to renewable energy sources, and shifts to more energy-efficient consensus mechanisms.

Many blockchains, including Ethereum, have transitioned from PoW to **Proof of Stake (PoS)**, which uses far less electricity. Ethereum's 2022 transition cut its energy use by over **99%**.

Mining operations are increasingly powered by renewable **energy** such as hydro, solar, and wind. Equipment manufacturers are developing more efficient hardware, and some miners reuse excess heat or recycle outdated devices to limit electronic waste. Water usage is also a concern, as large amounts of water are needed to cool mining data centers, prompting further sustainability considerations.

Governments and regulators are encouraging **transparency and sustainable practices**, while scaling solutions like the **Lightning Network** reduce overall energy demand. Combined, these initiatives aim to make blockchain technology more energy-efficient and environmentally responsible, balancing growth with sustainability.

Tip: Choose cryptocurrencies and platforms that prioritize energy efficiency or use proof-of-stake systems. Supporting sustainable mining helps the planet while keeping your crypto investments responsible.

High Energy Consumption (PoW Mining)

Bitcoin's energy use depends on mining activity, hardware efficiency, and network changes. Mining rigs, especially ASIC (Application-Specific Integrated Circuits), require a constant electricity supply to perform the complex computations needed to secure the blockchain. Large-scale mining operations—data centers and mining farms—often run thousands of machines 24/7, consuming massive amounts of electricity.

The environmental impact of mining depends largely on the energy source. Estimates suggest Bitcoin mining emits around 37 megatons of carbon dioxide per year, comparable to the emissions of countries like New Zealand or Finland. These emissions contribute to global warming by trapping heat in the Earth's atmosphere.

If electricity comes from coal, natural gas, or other fossil fuels, mining directly increases carbon emissions. Some operations use renewable energy sources such as hydropower, solar, or wind, but these remain a small portion of total mining. Most mining is still powered by fossil fuels, making energy consumption a major environmental concern.

PoW Energy Efficiency Challenges

In PoW networks, as more miners join and mining becomes more complex, the energy required to mine new coins rises exponentially. Bitcoin also has a built-in event called "halving," which occurs roughly every four years. During halving, the reward miners receive for mining a new block is cut in half. This helps control the total supply of Bitcoin, which is capped at 21 million coins. Halving doesn't remove existing coins; it just slows the rate at which new coins enter the network.

As a result, mining becomes more challenging and energy-intensive. Each additional unit of computational work requires more electricity, leading to diminishing returns in energy efficiency. Only miners with energy-efficient hardware or access to affordable electricity can continue to mine profitably. Less efficient miners may be forced to shut down, which can temporarily reduce the overall network hash rate. This combination of halving and increasing mining difficulty ensures that Bitcoin's supply grows slowly and predictably, while rewarding those who can maintain efficient operations.

Inequality in Access to Clean Energy and Grid Stability

Many mining operations are in regions with cheap electricity, which often comes from fossil fuels. This gives an advantage to large mining operations, while smaller or individual miners may struggle to compete. Some areas with abundant renewable energy—like parts of Iceland, Canada, and Norway—are attracting miners, but these green-energy regions still make up a small portion of the overall mining power.

Large-scale mining can also stress local power grids, sometimes causing higher electricity prices and making it harder for regular consumers to access affordable energy. In extreme cases, governments have stepped in. For example, China banned crypto mining due to its high energy demand, which strained the grid and contributed to excessive carbon emissions.

Some blockchain networks are encouraging miners to use cleaner energy.

For instance, the "Chia Network" uses a Proof of Space and Time (PoST) mechanism, which relies on storage space rather than electricity-heavy computations, making it far more energy-efficient.

Additionally, organizations like the Bitcoin Mining Council promote renewable energy use, and some major mining operations are transitioning to hydropower and other clean sources.

Takeaway: Bitcoin mining uses massive amounts of energy, mostly from fossil fuels, which contributes to climate change. Supporting renewable energy and energy-efficient networks can reduce crypto's environmental impact and help level the playing field for smaller miners.

What is the Local Environmental Impact of PoW Mining?

Mining operations concentrated in specific regions can have noticeable local environmental effects. For example, some mining farms—especially those in areas with cheap electricity—use large amounts of water to cool their equipment, which can put pressure on local water supplies and surrounding ecosystems.

Pollution is another concern. In regions with weak environmental regulations, mining operations can generate local pollution if hardware is improperly disposed of or not recycled according to standards. Large-scale mining can also contribute to noise and electronic waste, further impacting communities near mining facilities.

Mining Hardware Lifespan

Mining hardware often becomes obsolete quickly, contributing to a growing electronic waste problem. **Mining rigs**—high-powered, specialized computer systems built solely to verify blockchain transactions—often become obsolete quickly, contributing to a growing electronic waste problem. These discarded machines can harm the environment if they are not properly recycled, as they often contain hazardous materials that require professional disposal.

In PoW mining, ASIC miners typically become outdated within a few years due to improvements in mining technology or increasing network difficulty. This rapid obsolescence means that large amounts of mining equipment are discarded rather than reused or recycled.

It is estimated that the global Bitcoin network generates over 30,700 tons of electronic waste each year—more than some countries produce. According to a December 2021 article, "Bitcoin's Growing E-Waste Problem" by Alex de Vries and Christian Stall, this figure could rise to more than 64,000 tons annually as mining continues to grow.

Takeaway: The environmental impact of cryptocurrency mining goes beyond electricity consumption. Because mining hardware has a short lifespan, it creates significant electronic waste. This reality emphasizes the need for responsible recycling and the shift toward more sustainable blockchain designs.

Chapter 8

Cryptocurrency Adoption

Involvement from companies, banks, or governments can signal legitimacy and influence prices. In September 2021, El Salvador became the first country in the world to officially adopt Bitcoin as legal currency alongside the U.S. dollar.

The government gave $30 in Bitcoin to every citizen who signed up for the program and encouraged its use for buying goods and services through a government-created digital wallet on smartphones. This historic experiment aimed to increase financial inclusion, attract investors, and foster innovation.

The decision faced opposition from some international organizations, like the International Monetary Fund, and public protesters. Critics cited Bitcoin's volatility and potential risks to El Salvador's economy. Supporters argued that Bitcoin could expand access to financial services for the 70% of Salvadorans who did not have a bank account before adoption, offering an alternative to traditional banking.

The outcomes have been mixed. El Salvador issued $1 billion in Bitcoin-backed bonds and began constructing a "Bitcoin City," attracting global attention and investors. However, financial losses and ongoing uncertainties have created pressure on the government to manage Bitcoin-related risks carefully.

Surveys show that a large majority of Salvadorans do not use Bitcoin in everyday transactions. In 2023, around 85–88% reported not using Bitcoin, and by 2024, roughly 92% said they did not transact with Bitcoin.

Bottom Line: Cryptocurrency is still in its infancy, and it has a lot of potential. However, adopting it as a national currency could spark skepticism, given its short history and inherent instability. Nevertheless, positive regulations can influence the cryptocurrency landscape favorably and facilitate its wider acceptance.

Cryptocurrency ATMs (Bitcoin ATMs)

Cryptocurrency ATMs, also called Bitcoin ATMs or BTMs, first appeared in 2013. They were introduced by Robocoin, a cryptocurrency company based in Las Vegas. The very first Bitcoin ATM was installed at Wave Coffee House in Vancouver, Canada, allowing customers to buy or sell Bitcoin in person using cash or debit cards.

Since then, companies like Bitcoin Depot, CoinFlip, and Coinbase have expanded the network globally. In 2025, there were more than 37,000 crypto ATMs worldwide, with roughly 31,300 in the United States alone, making it easier for users to exchange cash and cryptocurrencies.

Unlike traditional ATMs connected to banks, crypto ATMs are linked to cryptocurrency exchanges. Users can deposit cash to buy crypto or sell digital assets to receive cash.

The popularity of crypto ATMs has grown rapidly in the U.S., Europe, and Latin America, driven by rising adoption, efforts to increase financial inclusion, and the demand for convenient access to digital assets.

Operators follow regulations through Know Your Customer (KYC) and Anti-Money Laundering (AML) procedures, requiring users to verify their identity. Modern ATM machines are also expanding their functionality, offering services like bill payments and money transfers.

While cryptocurrency ATMs offer convenience, users must understand the risks involved. Unlike traditional banking ATMs, crypto ATMs do not provide deposit insurance or consumer protections. Transactions are irreversible, fees are often higher, and errors or scams can lead to permanent loss of funds. Being aware of these risks is critical for safe usage.

Some of the main risks include:

- **Higher Fees:** Crypto ATMs can charge 6–12% per transaction, significantly more than online exchanges.

- **Irreversible Transactions:** Sending crypto to the wrong address or QR code cannot be undone.

- **Security and Tampering Risks:** Machines from untrustworthy operators could be hacked or compromised.

- **Privacy Concerns:** KYC requirements mean personal information is collected and stored.

- **Physical Safety:** Using ATMs in poorly lit or unsecured areas could expose users to theft.

Tip: Always start with small transactions, verify the QR code/address carefully, check fees in advance, and use reputable machines in safe locations.

Real-World Applications and Market Trends

Crypto adoption is growing across industries, signaling wider acceptance of blockchain technology and digital currencies. Real-world applications now go beyond trading and payments, reaching gaming, retail, real estate, supply chains, healthcare, and even voting systems.

Payments and Financial Services

Crypto-friendly retailers and companies like Overstock, Shopify, and Starbucks accept digital currencies. Payment networks such as PayPal, Visa, and Mastercard allow merchants to accept Bitcoin, Ethereum, and stablecoins. Ripple (XRP) and Stellar (XLM) enable fast, low-cost international transfers.

Gaming and NFTs

Games like Axie Infinity, Decentraland, and The Sandbox reward players with cryptocurrency.

NFT marketplaces such as OpenSea, Rarible, and Magic Eden allow users to buy, sell, and verify ownership of digital collectibles.

Blockchain also ensures intellectual property rights for artists and musicians, automatically tracking royalties.

Retail, Rewards, and Loyalty Programs

Brands like Lolli and StormX give Bitcoin rewards for shopping online. Luxury brands such as Louis Vuitton use blockchain to verify product authenticity and reduce counterfeiting.

Supply Chain and Logistics

Blockchain improves transparency and traceability. IBM Food Trust and VeChain allow retailers to track product origins and movement.

Walmart uses blockchain to quickly trace contamination sources, improving food safety.

Healthcare and Data Security

Hospitals and health systems like Beth Israel Deaconess and Intermountain Healthcare use blockchain to securely store and share patient records.

Blockchain allows authorized doctors to access records without relying on paper, physical CDs, or faxed documents. Companies like BurstIQ and Medicalchain secure medical records for privacy and compliance.

Voting and Identity Verification

West Virginia piloted a blockchain-based mobile voting app for military personnel overseas, enhancing election security and transparency.

Microsoft is developing blockchain solutions for individuals to control personal identification data, allowing secure, verifiable access to services like background checks without sharing sensitive documents.

The Tokenization of Real Estate

One of the most exciting real-world applications emerging in the crypto space is **real estate tokenization**. This process involves taking ownership of a physical property—such as an apartment building or office complex—and representing it as digital tokens on a blockchain. While this approach is not yet mainstream, pilot programs and early offerings are already underway in several countries.

Tokenization allows a high-value property to be divided into thousands of smaller digital units, similar to how a company issues shares of stock. This means individuals can invest in **fractional ownership** of real estate, lowering the barrier to entry for an asset class that was traditionally limited to wealthy investors and large institutions. In return, token holders may earn a share of rental income and potentially benefit if the property's value increases over time.

However, because this market is still in its early stages, tokenized real estate comes with notable risks. One key challenge is **illiquidity**—real estate tokens are not as easy to buy or sell as publicly traded stocks, since trading platforms and active buyers are still limited.

Another concern is the evolving regulatory landscape, as laws governing digital ownership of physical property are still developing. This can create uncertainty if legal or operational issues arise.

While real estate tokenization has the potential to democratize property investing and reshape how real assets are bought and sold, investors should understand that it remains an **early-stage innovation** with higher regulatory and infrastructure risks than traditional real estate investments.

Institutional Tokenization: Moving Markets to the Blockchain

Beyond retail payments, global financial giants are now "tokenizing" traditional assets like government bonds, gold, and private equity. This process involves turning ownership of a traditional financial instrument into a digital token on a blockchain. In 2024 and 2025, firms like *BlackRock* and *Franklin Templeton* launched tokenized funds that allow investors to buy into government treasuries with the speed of a crypto transaction. Meanwhile, banks like *JPMorgan* and *HSBC* are piloting blockchain systems to move trillions of dollars in collateral to eliminate the days of paperwork and manual processing usually required in traditional finance. This shift signals that blockchain is no longer viewed solely as an alternative system—it is being developed as foundational infrastructure for some of the world's largest institutions.

The Institutional Pivot: DTCC and the NYSE

The shift toward a digital future is not limited to private banks; it has reached the very core of the U.S. financial infrastructure. The **Depository Trust & Clearing Corporation (DTCC)**—the "backbone" of Wall Street that settles nearly all U.S. stock trades—has launched a pilot program to tokenize real-world assets like U.S. Treasuries and ETFs. By 2026, this system is expected to allow for "around-the-clock" asset transfers and near-instant settlement.

Similarly, the **New York Stock Exchange (NYSE)** and **Nasdaq** have announced initiatives and regulatory filings to support future trading of tokenized securities.

These moves aim to eliminate the traditional two-day waiting period for stock trades (known as T+2) and replace it with **instant settlement** (known as T+0), to merge the 24/7 efficiency of crypto with the trust and regulation of the traditional stock market.

Bottom Line: Blockchain technology is far more than just the foundation for cryptocurrencies like Bitcoin and Ethereum; it is emerging as a complementary and potentially foundational layer of future financial infrastructure. While many initiatives remain in pilot stages, the growing involvement of institutions such as BlackRock, DTCC, and major global banks signals a long-term shift toward faster settlement, improved transparency, and more automated market processes. This evolution is not about creating new coins, but about modernizing how assets and data move across financial systems.

Government Adoption and Regulations

Central Bank Digital Currencies (CBDCs) and Regulation

According to the Atlantic Council's Central Bank Digital Currency (CBDC) Tracker, countries such as the Bahamas, Jamaica, and Nigeria have fully launched CBDCs. A CBDC is a digital version of a country's fiat currency—such as the dollar, euro, or yuan—that is issued, centralized, and controlled by a central bank, rather than operating on a decentralized blockchain like Bitcoin.

Other major economies are actively testing or piloting digital currencies. China continues to expand trials of its Digital Yuan, while the European Union and the United Kingdom are exploring their own national digital currency frameworks.

At the same time, many governments are updating tax laws to formally include cryptocurrency earnings, signaling growing recognition of digital assets within traditional financial systems.

In June 2023, a Reuters analysis found that 130 countries—representing roughly 98% of the global economy—were exploring or developing CBDCs, highlighting how quickly governments are moving in this space.

In the United States, digital asset policy has also evolved. On March 6, 2025, the U.S. government announced the creation of a **Bitcoin reserve**, marking a notable shift in how digital assets are viewed at the federal level. This move signaled growing institutional recognition of Bitcoin as a long-term strategic asset.

As crypto adoption grows, increased participation by businesses and governments has helped boost demand—but it has also brought **greater regulatory oversight**. These developments show how cryptocurrency and blockchain technology are becoming more integrated into real-world financial systems.

Regulatory Developments Shaping Crypto Markets

Regulation isn't just about government rules; it's about creating a safe environment for everyone to participate. The New York Department of Financial Services (NYDFS) is at the forefront of this effort with its "BitLicense" framework—widely considered the most rigorous crypto regulation in the world.

To earn this license, companies must meet strict requirements for cybersecurity, capital reserves, and consumer protection. The final rules were published in June 2025, creating the first comprehensive crypto regulatory framework in the U.S.

This high level of oversight has created a new demand for specialized professional roles. Modern crypto firms are now required to appoint a **Chief Information Security Officer (CISO)** and a **Compliance Officer** specifically trained in digital assets.

These experts often hold certifications like the **Certified Bitcoin Professional (CBP)** or the **Certified Anti-Money Laundering Specialist (CAMS)** to ensure that the "Automated Money Exchange Kiosks" we discussed earlier are not only efficient but also fully compliant with global financial laws.

In 2020, the Financial Action Task Force (FATF) required cryptocurrency exchanges to follow the same Anti-Money Laundering (AML) standards as traditional banks. As a result, Know Your Customer (KYC) requirements became **mandatory** on most platforms, making anonymous trading increasingly difficult.

The collapse of Terra-LUNA in 2022, which erased billions of dollars in value, triggered global calls for stronger oversight. In response, the European Union introduced MiCA (Markets in Crypto-Assets)—one of the world's first comprehensive crypto regulatory frameworks.

Around the same time, countries such as the United States, the United Kingdom, and Japan strengthened AML and KYC requirements for crypto exchanges. In the U.S., the Securities and Exchange Commission (SEC) increased enforcement actions against fraudulent Initial Coin Offerings (ICOs), an unregulated fundraising method that previously allowed projects to raise millions with little oversight.

In May 2024, the U.S. House of Representatives passed the Financial Innovation and Technology for the 21st Century Act (FIT21). The bill aims to clarify which regulatory agencies oversee different types of digital assets, reducing long-standing confusion in the U.S. crypto market.

A major shift followed in December 2025, when the Office of the Comptroller of the Currency (OCC) allowed U.S. national banks to act as intermediaries for cryptocurrency trading.

Under this guidance, banks can operate using a "riskless principal" model, meaning they match buyers and sellers without holding crypto on their balance sheets. This approach is expected to improve consumer protection by bringing crypto access into regulated banking environments.

Binance, the world's largest cryptocurrency exchange, has advised several governments on digital asset regulations and the potential establishment of national Bitcoin reserves.

Together, these developments show how collaboration between regulators, governments, and industry participants is shaping the next phase of global cryptocurrency adoption.

The Road Ahead

Cryptocurrency is no longer an experiment — it's a movement reshaping how we think about money, ownership, and trust. Whether you choose to invest, build, or simply observe, understanding crypto puts you ahead of the curve. The digital economy is evolving with or without us, but those who learn today will help influence tomorrow's financial world.

What role do you want to play in the future of the digital economy?

Online Resources

The following websites provide reliable information on digital assets, market data, project fundamentals, terminology, and industry developments. These resources can help readers conduct independent research and stay informed.

CoinMarketCap — https://coinmarketcap.com
A comprehensive cryptocurrency data platform that provides real-time prices, market capitalization rankings, trading volume, historical charts, and project summaries. It also includes information about exchanges, token supply, and trending assets.

CoinGecko — https://www.coingecko.com
An independent cryptocurrency data aggregator offering price tracking, market metrics, tokenomics details, developer activity indicators, and educational resources. CoinGecko also provides extensive information on decentralized finance (DeFi) projects and NFT markets.

Messari — https://messari.io
A research-focused platform that publishes in-depth reports, analytics, and data on digital assets, blockchain projects, and market trends. It is widely used for fundamental analysis and institutional-grade insights.

Glassnode — https://glassnode.com
An on-chain analytics provider that tracks blockchain activity such as transaction volume, wallet behavior, and network health. Its data is commonly used to assess market cycles and investor sentiment.

CryptoCompare —
https://www.cryptocompare.com

Offers market data, portfolio tracking tools, mining information, exchange comparisons, and industry research reports.

IntoTheBlock — https://www.intotheblock.com
Provides analytics combining on-chain data, derivatives metrics, and machine learning insights to evaluate market trends and asset behavior.

Santiment — https://santiment.net
Focuses on social sentiment, on-chain metrics, and behavioral analytics to help identify trends driven by investor psychology and market activity.

Project Research and Transparency

Etherscan — https://etherscan.io
A blockchain explorer for the Ethereum network that allows users to verify transactions, wallet balances, smart contracts, and token information directly on the blockchain.

Token Terminal — https://tokenterminal.com
Provides financial metrics for blockchain projects, including revenue, protocol usage, and valuation indicators similar to traditional equity analysis.

DefiLlama — https://defillama.com
Tracks total value locked (TVL) across DeFi protocols and provides insights into decentralized finance ecosystems across multiple blockchains.

News and Industry Updates

CoinDesk — https://www.coindesk.com
A major digital asset news outlet covering market developments, regulation, technology, and industry trends.

Cointelegraph — https://cointelegraph.com
Provides global news coverage on cryptocurrencies, blockchain technology, and Web3 developments.

The Block — https://www.theblock.co
Offers research, data dashboards, and news focused on institutional developments and market structure.

Educational Resources and Terminology

Investopedia — https://www.investopedia.com
Provides clear explanations of financial and cryptocurrency terminology, investment concepts, and market mechanics.

Binance Academy — https://academy.binance.com
A free educational platform offering articles and guides on blockchain technology, trading concepts, security practices, and digital asset fundamentals.

Security and Risk Awareness

Chainalysis — https://www.chainalysis.com
A blockchain analytics company that publishes research on illicit activity, scams, and financial crime trends in the cryptocurrency ecosystem.

Scam Sniffer — https://scamsniffer.io
Tracks phishing attacks and malicious websites targeting
crypto users, helping identify emerging threats.

Author Disclaimer: *The inclusion of a website or
organization does not constitute an endorsement. Readers
should conduct independent research and exercise caution
when using any online resource.*

Key Terms

Term	Description
Altcoins	Additional virtual coins (tokens) introduced after Bitcoin (e.g., Litecoin, Ripple, Ethereum).
ASICs (Application-Specific Integrated Circuits)	Specialized hardware designed solely for cryptocurrency mining.
Bartering	Trading a good or service directly for another good or service without using money.
Bitcoin (BTC)	The first digital asset, created in 2009 by Satoshi Nakamoto (a pseudonymous entity).
Bitcoin Halving	An event in which the reward for mining new blocks is cut in half, reducing the rate at which new coins are created and increasing scarcity.
Blockchain	A distributed ledger system that records transactions in consecutive blocks, creating a secure, transparent record.
Central Bank Digital Currency (CBDC)	A digital currency issued and controlled by a central bank. Examples include China's Digital Yuan.
Centralized Exchanges (CEXs)	Platforms operated by a company that match buyers and sellers for cryptocurrency trading.

Cold Wallet	A cryptocurrency wallet not connected to the internet, used for secure storage.
Crypto Exchange	A business that allows users to trade cryptocurrencies for fiat or other cryptocurrencies.
Cryptocurrency	Digital tokens used as a medium of exchange. Their value is determined by what people are willing to pay.
Cryptocurrency Market	The global marketplace where cryptocurrencies are bought, sold, and traded.
Currency	A medium of exchange that represents value.
Decentralization	A system where decision-making authority is distributed rather than controlled by a single entity.
Decentralized Currency	A currency that operates without a bank or central authority.
Decentralized Exchange (DEX)	A peer-to-peer platform for trading crypto without intermediaries.
Decentralized Marketplace	A blockchain-based marketplace where users trade directly without middlemen.
Denial-of-Service (DoS) Attack	An attack intended to make a network or service temporarily unavailable.
Digital Art	Artwork created using digital technology.

Digital Asset	Any digital representation of value.
Digital Coins	A cryptocurrency unit that can operate independently.
Digital Currency	Currency that exists only digitally, not physically.
Digital Wallet	A software or hardware tool for storing, sending, and receiving cryptocurrencies.
Distributed Ledger	A ledger where data is stored across multiple decentralized nodes.
Fiat Currency	Government-issued legal tender (e.g., USD, EUR) backed by a central authority.
FOMO (Fear of Missing Out)	Anxiety that one might miss out on a profitable opportunity.
Fork / Hard Fork / Soft Fork	*Fork*: When a blockchain splits into two separate chains. *Hard Fork*: Permanent split creating a new chain. *Soft Fork*: Backward-compatible change to blockchain rules.
Hash	The output of a cryptographic algorithm used to secure and verify data.
Hot Wallet	A cryptocurrency wallet connected to the internet for easy access.
Initial Coin Offering (ICO)	A fundraising method where new digital coins are sold to raise capital.

Initial Dex Offering (IDX)	A decentralized alternative to an ICO.
Initial Public Offering (IPO)	When a company raises funds by offering shares to the public (analogous to crypto fundraising).
Instant Order	A trade executed immediately at the current market price.
Limit Order	A trade executed only at a specified price or better.
Liquidity / Illiquidity	*Liquidity*: Ease of selling an asset quickly. *Illiquidity*: Difficulty in selling an asset without losing value.
Market Capitalization (Cap)	The total market value of a cryptocurrency, calculated by multiplying total supply by current price.
Masternode	A blockchain node performing specialized functions beyond transaction validation, earning rewards.
Meme Coins	Crypto tokens created as a joke or meme, often highly speculative.
Miners	Individuals or groups who validate transactions and maintain the blockchain.
Mining / Mining Rig / Mining Farm	Using computational power to solve puzzles, validate transactions, and earn new coins. A mining rig is the equipment used; a mining farm is a large setup of rigs.

Node	A participant in a blockchain network that stores and validates data.
Non-Fungible Token (NFT)	A unique digital asset representing ownership or authenticity of an item, verified on the blockchain.
Oracle	An agent that provides real-world data to smart contracts for execution under specific conditions.
Peer-to-Peer (P2P)	Direct trading between two users without intermediaries.
Phishing	A scam where attackers impersonate trusted entities to steal sensitive information.
Pig Butchering	A long-term crypto scam where fraudsters build trust before tricking victims into fake investments.
Private Key / Secret Key	A code that grants control over a cryptocurrency wallet.
Proof of Work (PoW)	A consensus mechanism where miners solve energy-intensive puzzles to validate transactions.
Proof of Stake (PoS)	A consensus mechanism where validators lock tokens to confirm transactions and secure the blockchain.

Pseudonymous	Using an alias or identifier instead of a real legal name for transactions.
Public Ledger	A transparent record of all blockchain transactions accessible to the network.
Pump-and-Dump	A scheme where crypto prices are artificially inflated before being sold off by fraudsters.
Rug Pull	A scam where project developers abandon a project and steal investors' funds.
Seed Phrase	A sequence of words that allows access and recovery of a cryptocurrency wallet.
Slashing	A penalty in PoS systems for validators who break network rules.
Smart Contract	A program that automatically executes agreements on the blockchain without intermediaries.
Staking	Locking tokens in a PoS network to validate transactions and earn rewards.
Stop-Loss Order	An order to automatically sell an asset when it reaches a certain price to limit losses.
Stablecoin	A cryptocurrency designed to maintain a stable value, usually pegged to fiat currency.
Token	A digital unit providing access or utility within a crypto system.

Tokenization	The transcription of an asset into a digital token on a blockchain or a digital platform with similar properties. In this context, tokens can represent ownership, rights, or claims on tangible or intangible assets and may be traded or transferred on digital platforms.
Tokenomics	The study of rules governing a cryptocurrency's creation, supply, and economic incentives.
Two-Factor Authentication (2FA)	A security method requiring two forms of verification to access an account.
AML (Anti-Money Laundering)	Rules and procedures used by financial institutions to detect and prevent illegal money from entering the financial system.
FATF (Financial Action Task Force)	A global body that creates rules and recommendations to help countries fight money laundering and terrorist financing.
KYC (Know Your Customer)	The identity-verification process used by banks and crypto platforms to confirm who their customers are.

Further Reading

White Papers

Nakamoto, S. (2008). *Bitcoin: A Peer-to-Peer Electronic Cash System*. Available at bitcoin.org

Eyal, I., & Sirer, E. G. (2014). *Majority Is Not Enough: Bitcoin Mining Is Vulnerable*. arXiv

Narayanan, A., & Clark, J. (2017). *Bitcoin's Academic Pedigree*. ACM Queue

Mejia, D. D. (2025, April 24). *A Crypto Asset Risk Classification Methodology: CARR (Crypto Asset Risk Rating)*. Potestas Solutions LLC

Books & Magazines

Lewis, A. (2018). *The Basics of Bitcoins and Blockchains*.

Dawkins, R. (1976). *The Selfish Gene*.

Bashir, I. (2023). *Mastering Blockchain: Unlocking the Power of Cryptocurrencies, Smart Contracts, and Decentralized Applications (4th ed.)*. Packt Publishing

Captain BTC. (2022). *The Pillars of Tokenomics & the ve Token Model*.

Articles

Royal, J. (2025). *Best Bitcoin ETFs: Top funds for buying Bitcoin. Bankrate*

Asgari, N. (2024). *Crypto has designs on real estate. Financial Times*

Berke, A. (2017). *How safe are blockchains? It depends. Harvard Business Review*

Lewis, A. (2015). *A gentle introduction to blockchain technology. Bits on Blocks*

Wagh, A. (2022). *6 things you'll need for a successful crypto mining operation. Digital Conqueror*

Smith, C. (2024). *Enter the world of decentralized finance (DeFi). Trade Hexa*

Dev Duniya. (2025). *How to become a blockchain developer in 2025*

Oguntona, J. (2022). *Centralized vs. decentralized cryptocurrency exchanges. CryptoConsultz*

Hasenstab, G. (2025). *Blockchain tokenization and property ownership. Medium*

EFE. (2025). *Bitcoin use in El Salvador reaches historic low. El Economista*